Read & Understand

Grade 5

WITH LEVELED TEXTS

Writing: Delana Heidrich
Kathleen Simpson
Tekla White
Content Editing: Barbara Allman
De Gibbs
Copy Editing: Laurie Westrich
Art Direction: Cheryl Puckett
Cover Design: Liliana Potigian
Illustration: Len Borozinski
Design/Production: Yuki Meyer
John D. Williams

EMC 3445
Evan-Moor®
Helping Children Learn

Visit
teaching-standards.com
to view a correlation
of this book.
This is a free service.

Correlated to State and Common Core State Standards

Congratulations on your purchase of some of the finest teaching materials in the world.

For information about other Evan-Moor products, call 1-800-777-4362, fax 1-800-777-4332, or visit our website, www.evan-moor.com.

18 Lower Ragsdale Drive, Monterey, CA 93940-5746. Printed in USA.

CPSIA: Printed by McNaughton & Gunn, Saline, MI USA.[3/2017]

Contents

How to Use This Book

The Stories

The stories in this book include fiction, realistic fiction, science fiction, nonfiction, biographies, and folk tales. With Lexile® scores ranging from 720 to 970, the reading levels span mid-fourth grade to mid-sixth grade.

Select a Story

Before selecting a story, determine how you will use the story.
Each story can be used

- as a directed lesson, with either an individual student or a group of students reading at the same level;
- by partners reading together; or
- for independent reading practice in the classroom or at home.

Preview the Story

1. Reproduce the story and give a copy to each student.
2. Discuss any vocabulary that might be difficult to decode or understand.
3. Have the students think about the title of the story and look at the picture or pictures to help them predict what the story is about.
4. Help students relate their prior knowledge and experience to the story.

Read the Story

A single story can be read for more than one purpose. You might first read the story for instructional purposes, and then have partners read the story again to improve comprehension and fluency. At a later time, you can use the story for independent reading. Each purpose calls for a different degree of story difficulty.

The Skill Pages

The four pages of reproducible activities that follow each story cover a variety of essential reading skills. The Skills Chart on page 5 provides an overview of the skills practiced in the activities. Each activity is suitable for either group instruction or independent practice.

Group Instruction

1. Reproduce the activity page for each student.
2. Make a transparency of the activity or write its content on the board.
3. Introduce the skill and guide students through the lesson.
4. Have students complete the activity as the group works through the lesson.

Independent Practice

Although many students will read the same story, they may each need to practice different skills. Assign the activities that are the most appropriate for each student's needs.

1. Be sure that the activity practices skills that have already been introduced to the student.
2. Review the directions and be sure that the student understands the task.
3. Go over the completed assignment with the student to assess his or her need for further practice.

Vietnamese Holidays

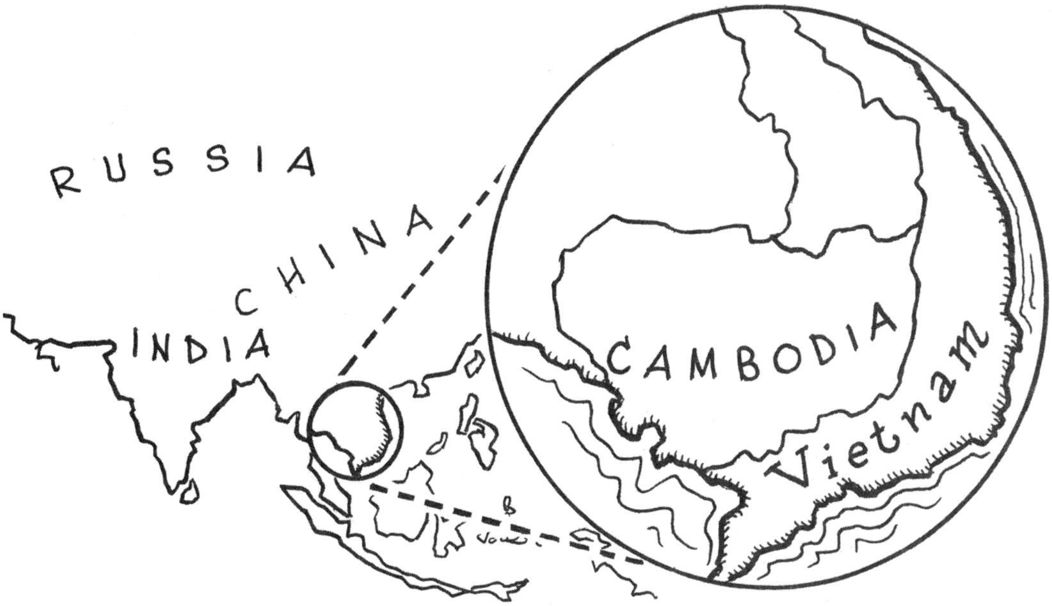

The Vietnamese celebrate many holidays each year. Some are days set aside to honor ancestors and their spirits. One is an incense ceremony day. There is also a long list of national holidays. Almost every Vietnamese holiday is celebrated with parades, prayers, flowers, fireworks, and special foods.

During a particular festival in autumn, children carry star lanterns in a parade. Everyone admires the harvest moon and enjoys moon cakes, which are special pastries filled with sesame or bean paste.

Every year, Buddhists celebrate the birthday of their founder, Buddha. During the celebration, captive birds and fish are set free in his honor.

One of the most important holidays in Vietnam is Tet. It is the Vietnamese New Year, and it signals the beginning of spring. Almost everyone in Vietnam celebrates this national holiday.

Tet takes place on different dates in January or February and lasts from three to seven days. It begins on the first day of the lunar year. Because the date depends on the cycles of the moon, Tet doesn't begin on the same date every year.

Before Tet begins, people clean their homes and decorate them with spring blossoms. Banners and lights are hung outdoors. During the celebration, people try to be very kind to each other. It's important for them to settle arguments that have taken place during the year.

Tet is a time to remember ancestors. An altar with pictures of the ancestors is arranged in the home. On New Year's Eve, food is placed on the altar along with candles and incense. The family invites the spirits of their ancestors to share the New Year's Eve dinner. The kitchen god is honored, too, with a special offering to make him happy. At the end of each year, this god is thought to give reports about the family to the Jade Emperor in heaven. If the kitchen god is pleased, the family believes he will praise them.

At midnight on New Year's Eve, families pray for good health and good fortune in the new year. Strings of loud firecrackers are set off to chase away evil spirits.

On the first day of the New Year, people go to temples and pagodas and pray to the gods of their religions. They pray for their ancestors and for a good new year. Children receive presents of red envelopes with money inside, and families enjoy treats made of preserved fruits and lotus seeds.

The Vietnamese believe that the first visitor to the house during Tet brings good luck or bad luck for the coming year, so the family takes great care to invite a special person who will bring them good fortune.

Many small villages in the hill country celebrate Tet with the traditional songs and dances of their regions. They also have special New Year activities, such as horse races or wrestling matches.

A variety of special holiday foods are served during Tet. Some favorites are noodles, fruits, sweet rice cakes with beans, and dumplings filled with pork and green beans. After the Tet celebrations are over, it's time to plant rice and other crops. Spring has officially arrived.

Name ____________________

Questions About *Vietnamese Holidays*

1. Why doesn't Tet begin on the same date each year?

____

____

2. How does a Vietnamese family honor its ancestors during Tet?

____

____

3. Why are offerings set out for the kitchen god on New Year's Eve?

____

____

4. Fill in the blanks using words from the story.

   a. Tet takes place in the month of ____________ or ____________.

   b. Tet lasts from ____________ to ____________ days.

   c. During Tet, it's important to be ____________ to everyone and to settle ____________.

   d. Before Tet, homes are ____________ and then ____________ with spring ____________.

5. Why is it important to invite a special guest to visit during Tet?

____

____

____

Name ______________________

Vocabulary

A. Write each word below on the line next to its definition.

incense	Tet	national	preserved	lotus	cycle
spirits	altar	ancestor	ceremony	pagoda	lunar

1. a place where some people in Vietnam go to pray ______________________
2. a substance that produces a sweet smell when it is burned ______________________
3. a relative who lived long ago ______________________
4. having to do with the moon ______________________
5. ghosts ______________________
6. a water plant that produces a seed that can be eaten ______________________
7. a place to pray and leave offerings ______________________
8. belonging to a country ______________________
9. a religious or public activity with a special purpose ______________________
10. a period of time or an event that is repeated many times ______________________
11. processed to last a long time ______________________
12. the name of the New Year celebration in Vietnam ______________________

B. List six types of food mentioned in the story.

______________________ ______________________

______________________ ______________________

______________________ ______________________

Name ____________________

Find the Words

Find these words from the story in the word search puzzle and circle them.

celebrate	firecrackers	fortune	holiday	honor	moon
parade	prayers	rice	sesame	spring	temples

m	r	h	v	c	r	m	p	a	r	a	d	e	o
p	j	o	i	p	t	b	t	g	t	p	m	z	n
c	e	l	e	b	r	a	t	e	u	a	o	b	t
x	a	i	t	a	r	a	j	q	s	l	o	a	r
p	l	d	n	t	i	n	y	e	f	e	n	l	h
k	t	a	r	n	c	v	s	e	o	t	s	i	g
z	l	y	m	g	e	r	s	p	r	i	n	g	t
t	e	m	p	l	e	s	z	k	t	s	l	m	e
s	o	l	g	m	p	w	e	r	u	m	o	k	s
t	c	w	e	x	l	r	h	o	n	o	r	s	t
f	i	r	e	c	r	a	c	k	e	r	s	n	h

Choose three words from the word search. Write each word in a sentence about Vietnam.

1. ______________________________

____

2. ______________________________

____

3. ______________________________

____

Name ____________________

Main Topics and Details

Write details under each of these topics from the story.
Write one detail next to each letter.

I. `Autumn Festival

A. ____________________

B. ____________________

C. ____________________

II. Buddha's Birthday

A. ____________________

B. ____________________

III. The First Day of Tet

A. ____________________

B. ____________________

C. ____________________

D. ____________________

E. ____________________

IV. Altars

A. ____________________

B. ____________________

C. ____________________

D. ____________________

V. Kitchen God

A. ____________________

B. ____________________

C. ____________________

The Gift

Great-Grandma took care of me when I was little. Now it's my turn to help her. She lives in a small house next door to ours. She eats dinner with us almost every evening, and Mom drives her to appointments and takes her shopping. She can do some of her own cleaning, but Mom and I do most of it. Because Mom has to be at work during the week, it's up to me to help G-G-Ma (that's what I call her) after school. Sometimes, I want to be with my friends or just watch TV after school, but then I remember that G-G-Ma used to give up time with her friends to take care of me.

I like talking to G-G-Ma. She tells me what life was like when she was growing up. She's also told me some funny stories about Mom. The best part is that she always has time to listen to me, laugh at my jokes, and give me hugs when I need them. She even throws in extra hugs when nothing is wrong.

Today is a special day. It's G-G-Ma's ninety-first birthday, and Mom and I have planned a surprise. Last night, we baked a cake, and when Mom gets home from work, she'll cook G-G-Ma's favorite dinner. I wanted to give G-G-Ma the perfect gift, but I couldn't find anything. Mom and I went shopping for a gift last Saturday, but nothing seemed quite right. G-G-Ma doesn't need another sweater or an apron, and she has enough towels and clothes to last another ninety-one years. She also has lots of knickknacks and figurines around the house, and I know she doesn't want any more because they are hard to dust. So Mom and I came home empty-handed. I made G-G-Ma a card and wrote a poem to go with it. Mom said that was enough, but I wished that I had found something really special—something that would make G-G-Ma happy.

I unlocked the door.

"I'm home from school," I called as I entered the house, but there wasn't any answer. I went into the kitchen and saw G-G-Ma sitting at the kitchen table, watching a tiny orange kitten eat scraps of leftover chicken.

"Oh, hello, Sally. The poor thing looked lost and hungry," G-G-Ma said. "I heard her crying outside. Somebody probably just went off and left her."

The kitten finished the food and scratched around.

"I'll take her back out," I said. I picked up the kitten and put her outside the kitchen door.

"It's better to leave her there," G-G-Ma said, but she sounded worried. "I can't take care of a kitten anymore—an old lady like me. I can't take care of myself sometimes. Maybe she'll find a home. She's a lot like my Belle, you know—the same color."

I remember how much G-G-Ma had loved Belle. That cat used to follow her everywhere. She played with the broom when G-G-Ma swept the floor. She rolled spools of thread all over the house. She even slept at the foot of G-G-Ma's bed. Sometimes, G-G-Ma talks about Belle like she's still here.

We heard the kitten meowing and scratching at the door. G-G-Ma got up and walked to the door.

"It's hard to turn anything away when it needs your help," she said, putting her hand on the doorknob. "But I can't take care of a kitten."

I put my arm around G-G-Ma. "I'll find a home for it," I said. Then I opened the door to let the kitten back in.

G-G-Ma sat in the chair again, and I put the kitten in her lap. It batted at her fingers a little and then curled up. G-G-Ma petted the kitten and laughed.

"I'd forgotten how soft a kitten is," she said, smiling.

I wished that I could keep the kitten, but Mom said "one pet," and I know she meant it! I already have a big dog that has too much energy. I have to keep the dog away from G-G-Ma so he doesn't knock her down. Most of my friends have pets already, too, but I'm going to have to figure out something.

"I'll be back in a few minutes, G-G-Ma," I said.

I went to my house and called Mom. I told her about the kitten—and then I told her my plan. At first, she didn't like it, but I kept talking and finally talked her into it. I quickly returned to G-G-Ma's house. While we were waiting for Mom, I helped G-G-Ma tie a button on a string and watched her dangle it for the kitten to play with.

Mom arrived at about 5:30 with her arms full of shopping bags. I helped her set them down, and she went over to hug G-G-Ma.

"Happy birthday, G-G-Ma," Mom said.

"Oh goodness, Martha, I'd forgotten all about it," G-G-Ma replied, never taking her eyes off the kitten.

"Look at this sweet little kitten, Martha," she continued. "Watch how it goes after the button. Sally helped me make this toy. You know my fingers aren't too good at putting things together anymore. I know I can't keep the kitten, but it sure has brightened my day. Sally says she'll find a home for it."

"She already has," Mom said. She went to the kitchen counter and pulled a bag of cat food out of one of the shopping bags.

"You can feed the kitten this dry food when she needs it," Mom said, placing the bag of food on the table in front of G-G-Ma, "and Sally will give it some canned food every day when she comes over. I also brought some litter and a litter box, bowls for food and water, and some toys. The kitten is your birthday present! And we'll both help you take care of it."

G-G-Ma started to cry, but I knew it wasn't because she was sad. Mom gave her a hug, and I gave her a tissue. Then I unloaded all the cat supplies Mom had brought.

"I'm bringing dinner over here tonight," Mom told G-G-Ma, "so get ready to celebrate! Sally can come help me carry the food when she gets everything set up for the kitten, and tomorrow, we'll make an appointment with a veterinarian for a kitten checkup."

Mom picked up the kitten. "I've missed Belle, too," she said.

"And I think I'll call her Little Belle," said G-G-Ma with a smile, as Mom handed the kitten back to her.

I guess we had done it after all. We had given G-G-Ma the perfect gift.

Name ____________________

Questions About *The Gift*

1. What did Sally like about helping her great-grandmother?

2. What kind of surprise had Sally and her mother planned for G-G-Ma's birthday?

3. Why couldn't Sally find a special gift for G-G-Ma?

4. Why do you think G-G-Ma told Sally that it was better to leave the kitten outside?

5. Why couldn't Sally keep the kitten?

6. How did Sally finally manage to give G-G-Ma the perfect birthday gift? How did Sally's mother contribute to the gift?

Name ______________________________

The Gift

Vocabulary Crossword

Use the words in the word box to complete the crossword puzzle.

Word Box

- appointment
- birthday
- brightened
- celebrate
- counter
- dangle
- energy
- figurine
- kitten
- litter
- spools
- supplies
- surprise
- tissue

Down

1. a kitchen work surface
3. made more enjoyable or appealing
4. items needed for a specific purpose
5. a young cat
6. the anniversary of the day a person was born
7. an unexpected action or event
9. soft, thin paper that readily absorbs liquids
10. to hang freely
11. material used to absorb waste from a house cat

Across

2. small cylinders used to hold thread
8. a scheduled time to be at a certain place or to meet with a certain person
12. a small statue of a person or an animal
13. the source of power for action or physical activity
14. to honor with a party or other special activities

Name ______________________________

Compound Words

A **compound word** combines two shorter words into one longer word with a single meaning. The combined words can be **closed** or **hyphenated**.

Examples: basketball (closed compound)
vice-president (hyphenated compound)

Look for compound words in the story and underline them. Write the correct compound word on the line next to each definition below.

1. ______________________ part of a door
2. ______________________ all around
3. ______________________ saved for another meal
4. ______________________ without anything
5. ______________________ small, decorative objects
6. ______________________ your parent's grandmother
7. ______________________ not indoors
8. ______________________ on certain occasions
9. ______________________ an age
10. ______________________ a yearly health exam

To and *Too*

The homophones **to** and **too** are pronounced the same, but they have different spellings, different uses, and different meanings.

Use the correct homophone to complete each sentence below.

1. Ali likes ________ read mystery books.
2. Eating ________ much candy might give you a stomachache.
3. Candy can harm your teeth, ________.
4. Tom rides his bicycle ________ school sometimes.

Name ____________________

Write About It

Write about something you either gave or received that seemed to be "the perfect gift." Tell how your experience was similar to or different from the situation in the story.

Amazing Ants!

Ants can be found in most parts of the world. Sometimes, we even find them in our kitchens! We may not like streams of ants marching through our homes, but we have to admire the way they work together.

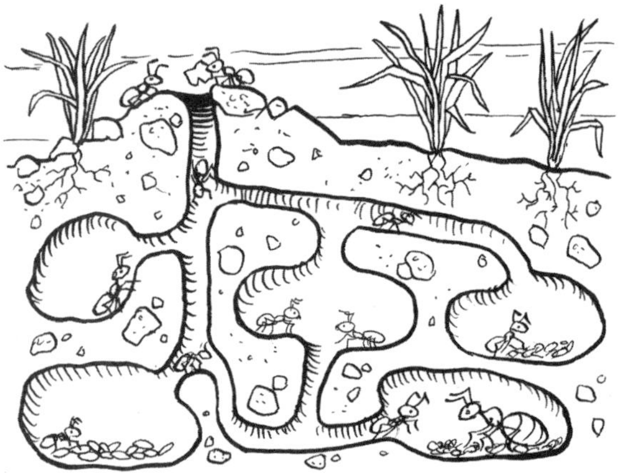

Ants live in communities called *colonies*. All the ants in a colony take care of each other, and they all have special jobs. Most of them are worker ants. Some workers clean and feed the queen. The queen lays all the eggs. Other workers care for the eggs and the larvae. Many worker ants go out each day to collect food. Some stay underground and take care of or enlarge the colony's living quarters.

Some ants are farmers. They carve out an enormous underground colony, where they farm fungi for the community to eat. First, leafcutters carry chunks of leaves back to the colony. Then, chewers grind the leaves into a yellow paste. Other ants spread the paste inside the colony's underground rooms. The paste fertilizes the fungi and helps them grow. The ants take good care of their crops to keep their food supply growing.

Some ants are herders. They take care of aphids. The aphids are another source of food for the ants. Herders shelter these tiny insects in winter and take them to plants when the weather is warmer. Then they milk the aphids by stroking the sides of the insects. The stroking causes the aphids to give off a sticky sap called *honeydew*. The ants lick up the sap and carry it back to the colony. The honeydew may be fed to other ants or stored for later use.

A very special group of ants guards the colony and lets only the ants that live there enter. Ants that don't belong to the community will try to kidnap larvae and then raise them to be slaves.

Ants build many kinds of homes for their communities, but most ants build their homes underground. Worker ants tunnel through the ground, building subterranean rooms. Sometimes, they dig down as deep as a one-story house. The ants move the earth one grain at a time! Often, their home is solar-heated. The ants build a tunnel under a rock. When the rock is warmed by the sun, the rooms of the tunnel stay warm and dry.

Some ants build mounds above ground. The mounds can be as tall as 5 feet (1.5 meters)—or even higher! To build these kinds of homes, ants dig up grains of wet soil from the ground and carry them to the mound. Sometimes, they pack the mud around blades of grass to make the walls of the mound stronger. They may also bring pine needles to the mound for a roof.

In South American rainforests, ants carry mud from the ground to a tree branch. They pack the mud around the branch and then tunnel into the mud ball to make their living quarters. The ants also gather seeds and plant them in the mud. Roots sprout and twist around through the mud, making it strong so heavy rains won't wash it away. When the plants in the mud ball bloom, they provide food for the ants.

Carpenter ants tunnel into wood to make their homes. They can be found in fence posts, tree stumps, and even houses. These ants can do a lot of damage. Some ants don't like to build or tunnel, so they make their homes in bamboo or other hollow plants.

Harvester ants clear away weeds and grass from around their houses to make "roads." They use the roads to more quickly bring home the food that they gather.

One type of ant actually chews leaves, wood, and flowers to make a paper house. The ants' saliva mixes with the plants as they chew and forms a paste. The ants shape the paste into a house, and it dries like paper.

Ants are truly hardworking insects. Like all insects, they have six legs, three body parts, a pair of antennae, and a hard exoskeleton. Ranging from only about $\frac{1}{12}$ of an inch to 1 inch (2 to 25 millimeters) long, ants are also very small insects. For animals their size, however, ants are amazing!

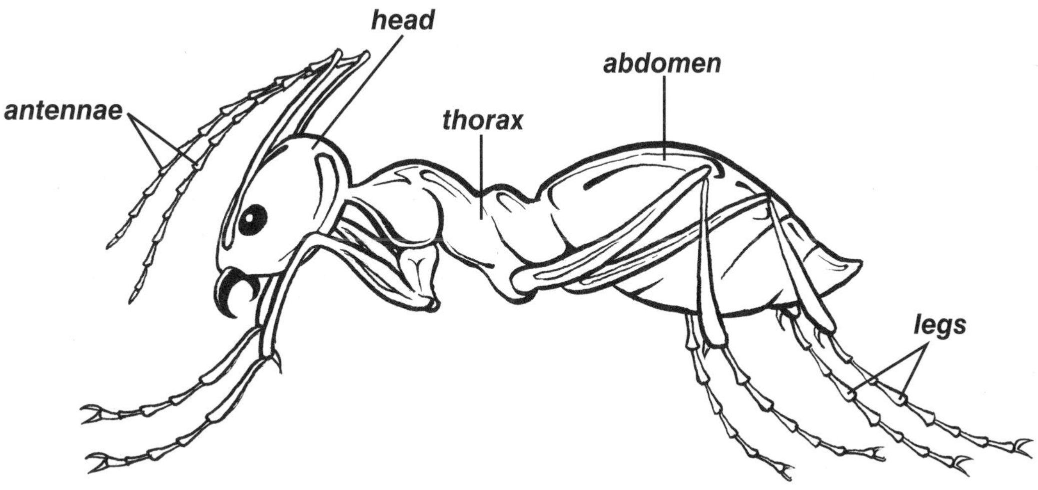

Name ______________________

Questions About *Amazing Ants!*

1. What are three of the jobs done by a colony's worker ants?

____

____

____

2. What do ants grow in their underground farms and how do they take care of their crops?

____

____

____

3. Why are aphids important to some ants?

____

4. What is honeydew? Where does it come from?

____

____

____

5. Why does an ant colony have guards?

____

____

____

6. Where do ants that don't tunnel or build make their homes?

____

Name ______________________________

What and Where

Write the letter of the type of ant or ant home on the line next to the correct description.

a. carpenter	_____	collects food for the colony
b. mud ball	_____	tunnels dug deep in the ground
c. herder	_____	grows fungi for the community to eat
d. leafcutter	_____	formed around a branch in the rainforest
e. mound	_____	clears away weeds and grass to make "roads"
f. shaped "paper"	_____	lays eggs
g. subterranean rooms	_____	gathers plant material to make fertilizer
h. harvester	_____	plant material mixed with saliva
i. worker	_____	a tunnel under a rock
j. solar-heated nest	_____	tunnels into wood to make its home
k. farmer	_____	strokes aphids to collect honeydew
l. queen	_____	grinds leaves into a yellow paste
m. guard	_____	a pile of wet soil above the ground
n. chewer	_____	protects larvae

Cause and Effect

Write the letter of each **cause** on the line next to the correct **effect**.

a. Harvester ants make roads.	_____	They take honeydew to the colony.
b. Carpenter ants tunnel into wood.	_____	They live in strong mounds.
c. Herders stroke the sides of aphids.	_____	They damage people's homes.
d. Some ants chew leaves and wood.	_____	The colony gets food more quickly.
e. Ants pack mud around grass.	_____	They live in paper houses.

Name ______________________________

Alphabetical Order

Write the words below in alphabetical order. Then find and circle each word in the word search puzzle.

subterranean	bamboo	herder	fungi
exoskeleton	saliva	larvae	chewer
honeydew	harvester	aphids	tunnel
leafcutter	carpenter	colony	mound

1. ______________________
2. ______________________
3. ______________________
4. ______________________
5. ______________________
6. ______________________
7. ______________________
8. ______________________
9. ______________________
10. ______________________
11. ______________________
12. ______________________
13. ______________________
14. ______________________
15. ______________________
16. ______________________

m	o	u	n	d	z	s	p	h	r	z	s
s	q	k	r	m	d	h	v	e	f	y	u
b	s	a	l	i	v	a	d	q	l	h	b
i	l	z	h	e	d	r	m	b	a	o	t
v	d	p	t	o	e	v	r	j	r	n	e
c	a	o	l	h	m	e	s	e	v	e	r
s	b	r	u	t	w	s	t	p	a	y	r
c	a	r	p	e	n	t	e	r	e	d	a
o	m	y	h	x	u	e	m	t	g	e	n
l	b	c	j	c	k	r	f	u	n	w	e
o	o	z	f	u	n	g	i	n	v	s	a
n	o	a	t	r	f	o	s	n	d	k	n
y	e	x	o	s	k	e	l	e	t	o	n
l	v	c	s	y	i	u	m	l	w	g	k

Name ______________________________

Synonyms

Find a synonym in the story for each word below and write it on the line. Use a dictionary if you need help understanding what these words mean.

1. kind ____________________
2. underground ____________________
3. excavate ____________________
4. expand ____________________
5. collect ____________________
6. gigantic ____________________
7. construct ____________________
8. abduct ____________________
9. rubbing ____________________
10. protects ____________________

Irregular Plurals

Most plural forms are made by adding **s** or **es**. The plural forms for the words listed below are made in different ways. Find the plural form in the story for each word and write it on the line.

1. fungus ____________________
2. larva ____________________
3. leaf ____________________
4. community ____________________

The Warrior and the Princess

The Legend of Popocatepetl and Ixtaccihuatl

In ancient times in the valley of Mexico, there lived a rich and powerful emperor. The emperor had many treasures. Colorful murals covered his palace, jewels and brilliant quetzal feathers covered his crown, but the treasure the emperor prized the most was his daughter, Ixtli (*eekst*-lee). Her long dark hair glistened like polished obsidian, and her eyes were a soft brown like the eyes of the deer that wandered through her garden. She was the most beautiful woman in the kingdom. Every young man who saw Ixtli wished to marry her, but no suitors pleased both Ixtli and her father.

One day, Prince Popo, a great warrior, traveled from his neighboring kingdom to the valley to search for a wife. When he saw Ixtli being carried to the marketplace on a litter, he thought, "She is as beautiful as people say. But beauty alone is not enough. I can love only a woman who has a kind and caring spirit."

Prince Popo disguised himself as a royal gardener so he could be near Ixtli to find out what she was really like. He watched her care for the animals in the garden. He saw that Ixtli often sent messengers with clothing and food to the poor people in the valley. Each day, Popo fell more in love with her. Finally, he could wait no longer.

Popo knelt before Ixtli.

"Forgive me, Princess," he said, "I am not a gardener at all. I am Prince Popo from the mountain kingdom. I have worked in your garden to be near you, and I have found that you are as kind as you are beautiful. I will love you forever."

Ixtli smiled at the young prince. She had fallen in love with the handsome gardener, but she hadn't told anyone because she knew her father would never let her marry a commoner. But a prince! Surely the emperor would agree to their marriage if it would bring her happiness.

Ixtli gave Popo the gold ring from her finger.

"You must speak to my father," she told him, "and show him my ring so he knows I have pledged my love to you."

"Oh, Princess, your love makes me so happy," said the prince. "I will go to my kingdom to tell my people of your great beauty. Then I will return to claim your hand."

Ixtli waited for the young prince to visit her father. Day after day, she watched for him. Months passed, and Ixtli grew thin and pale worrying about the prince. Had he been injured? Was he ill?

One afternoon as Ixtli sat by a window, one of her attendants burst into the room.

"Prince Popo is here!" the attendant exclaimed. "He has come with a chest full of treasures."

Ixtli ran to the visitor's room.

"I thought you would never return," she told the prince.

"I come from a poor mountain kingdom," Popo explained. "I could not return until I had treasures worthy of you. I have come today to ask your father to allow me to marry you."

"I will not hear of it!" stormed the emperor. "You are a prince of nothing. The man who marries my daughter must be worthy to rule my kingdom."

Ixtli ran sobbing from the room.

As more months passed, Ixtli pleaded with her father. Finally, seeing how unhappy his daughter was, the emperor sent for the young prince.

"My daughter's happiness is important to me," the emperor said to Popo. "I am willing to reconsider my decision if only to see her smile again. But you must show me that you are worthy of my daughter before I allow you to marry her. To prove that you are worthy, you will be my messenger to all the kingdoms that surround our valley."

One day, when Popo was carrying messages to a nearby kingdom, he saw soldiers marching toward the valley. He ran for two days through the forests and over the mountains to warn the emperor. The emperor's troops hadn't fought battles for many years. Popo knew that they would need a strong leader.

"I will command your soldiers," Popo told the emperor. "I have led my people against these same armies and defeated them."

"You have proven yourself a worthy messenger," said the emperor. "If you are a victorious warrior as well, you shall marry my daughter."

Popo and the emperor's soldiers fought the invaders for more than a year. When a messenger falsely reported that Popo had been killed, Ixtli died of grief. The same day she died, Popo and his army of warriors returned. Popo bowed before the emperor as he gave his report.

"There were many enemies," he said, "but we have won each battle. I will train every man in this kingdom so it will never be defeated."

The emperor, with great sadness over the death of his daughter, placed his crown on Popo's head.

"You have earned the kingdom, my son," he said quietly.

"I will accept the throne if I may marry Ixtli," said Popo.

The emperor led Popo to the room where Ixtli's lifeless body lay.

"She died this very day, thinking that you would never return," the emperor told Popo.

Popo turned away from the emperor and picked up Ixtli. He carried her to the hills overlooking the valley. Holding a torch, he watched over her, hoping that she would return to life. The snows came and covered the princess, but Popo stayed. He wouldn't leave her.

Today, you can still see Popo and Ixtli on the hills overlooking the valley of Mexico. The gods changed Ixtli into a snow-covered mountain called The Sleeping Woman. Popo, the brave and loyal warrior, became the smoking volcano that guards the mountain.

Name ___________________________

Questions About *The Warrior and the Princess*

1. Why was Ixtli unmarried?

2. Why did Popo pretend to be a gardener?

3. What did the prince find out about Ixtli while he was posing as a gardener?

4. Why did Prince Popo wait so long to ask the emperor if he could marry Ixtli?

5. Why did the emperor refuse, at first, to let Prince Popo marry his daughter?

6. How could you tell that Ixtli truly loved Prince Popo?

Name ______________________

Vocabulary Crossword

Use the words in the word box to complete the crossword puzzle.

Word Box

- attendant
- brilliant
- commoner
- emperor
- grief
- litter
- mural
- obsidian
- pledged
- quetzal
- suitor
- torch
- valley
- victorious
- warrior
- worthy

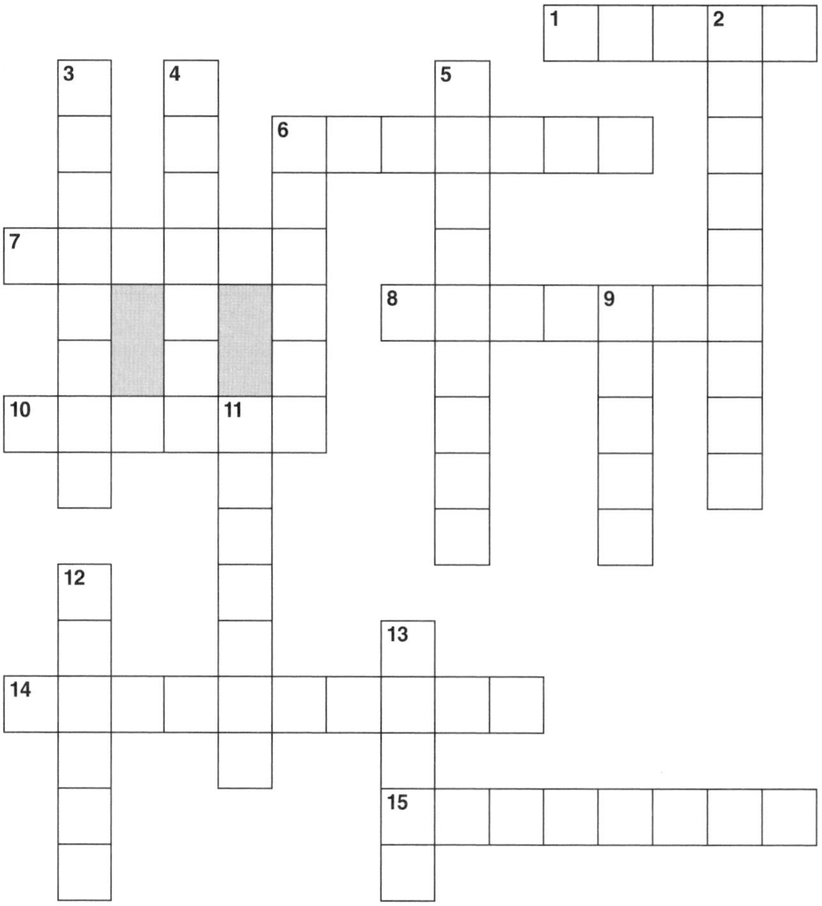

Across

1. a large picture painted on a wall
6. a soldier who fights in battles
7. a chair that rests on horizontal poles and is used to carry royalty from place to place
8. vowed or promised
10. a low area surrounded by hills or mountains
14. having won a war or a contest
15. a person who is not a noble or royalty

Down

2. a personal servant to a member of a royal family
3. a glassy black gemstone
4. a brightly colored tropical bird with long, magnificent tail feathers
5. shining
6. having value, deserving
9. great sadness
11. the ruler of a vast area and often many kingdoms
12. a man who pays attention to a woman, hoping to marry her
13. a large, flaming stick or club that is carried by hand

Name ______________________

The Warrior and the Princess

Describe the Characters

Write each word listed below on the line next to the story character or characters it best describes. You may use a word more than once.

beautiful	kind	brave	gentle	angry	caring	rich
worried	strong	powerful	loyal	worthy	grieving	loving

Emperor ______________________

Princess Ixtli ______________________

Prince Popo ______________________

Similes

A **simile** describes something by making a comparison using the word *like* or *as*.

1. Two similes describe Ixtli's beauty. Read the first simile below. Then find the second simile in the story and write it on the lines.

   Her long dark hair glistened like polished obsidian.

   ____

   ____

2. Write your own similes to complete these sentences.

   a. Prince Popo was as brave as ______________________.

   b. When Popo asked to marry Ixtli, the emperor was as angry as ______________________.

3. Similes often describe something by comparing it to an animal that is known for a particular trait. Complete each simile below using the name of an animal.

as strong as ______________________

as sly as ______________________

as stubborn as ______________________

as quiet as ______________________

works like ______________________

stings like ______________________

swims like ______________________

runs like ______________________

Name ________________________________

What Makes It a Legend?

A **legend** is a type of folk tale. Like all folk tales, it is a story that is passed down from generation to generation. Unlike most other folk tales, however, legends were once believed to be true but turned out to be fiction.

Some characteristics of legends are listed below. After each characteristic, write evidence from the story to show that it is a legend.

A legend...

1. takes place in the distant past.

____

____

2. is about real people, places, or events or is based on historical facts.

____

____

3. features lifelike, but often exaggerated, characters or events.

____

____

____

4. contains obstacles to be overcome.

____

____

5. explains something that exists in nature.

____

____

Beaks and Feathers

All birds, from tiny hummingbirds to the giant ostrich, are warmblooded vertebrates. All birds have two wings and two scaly legs. They also have a beak and feathers.

A bird's feet and its beak are adapted to its species' lifestyle. Some birds have perching toes. Others have webbed toes that help them swim and keep them from sinking into mud. Raptors, or birds of prey, have toes with sharp claws called *talons*. Raptors also have very strong beaks.

Birds' beaks vary even more than their feet. A seedeater's short beak is different from a woodpecker's sharp, pointed drill. Bug eaters, mud probers, and fish scoopers have beaks that help them find the kinds of foods they need.

As for their feathers, most birds molt, or lose their plumage, once or twice a year. Each time a bird molts, it sheds and then grows back all its feathers. The reason birds molt is to get rid of worn and damaged feathers and replace them with new, healthy ones. Most birds shed only a few feathers at a time, so they are still able to fly. But some birds, such as ducks and geese, molt all at once. These birds are actually flightless for a short time.

Here is a closer look at four fascinating species of birds and their remarkable beaks and feathers.

Owls

Owls are raptors that hunt at night. These meat eaters soar overhead looking for prey. They use their sharp talons to attack small ground animals and carry them off. Special fringed feathers on the edges of an owl's wings make the owl's flight silent. A mouse or a rabbit doesn't know the owl is near until the bird strikes.

With their large eyes, owls can see well in the dark. Owls can also see just as clearly far away as they can up close. Sometimes, an owl looks like it has eyes in the back of its head because it can turn its head around far enough to see directly behind itself. An owl's eyes don't move in the eye sockets, so the bird's head must turn to see anything that is not directly in front of it.

Flamingos

Thousands of flamingos flock together in warm saltwater lakes and rivers. The pink coloring in the shrimp and algae they eat passes through their bodies, turning their feathers various shades of pink.

The beak of this tall pink bird acts like a sieve. The flamingo pokes its head into the water, upside down, to look for shrimp in the mud. The shrimp that the flamingo scoops up stay inside the beak, while the water strains out through the lower part of the beak. The hook at the end of a flamingo's beak helps it build its nest of mud. Both males and females use their beaks to push the mud into a mound on which the female lays a single egg.

Pelicans

The beaks of these talented fishers have a pouch. The pouch stretches to hold the fish the pelican catches. White pelicans fish in groups, beating their wings to drive the fish into shallow water. There, the pelicans can easily scoop them up. Brown pelicans look for fish from the air. When a brown pelican spots a fish, it dives straight down into the water at high speed.

A pelican takes in water along with the fish it catches. A beak full of water and fish makes the pelican too heavy to fly. Before it can take off, it has to tip its head to the side to empty out the water. Then the pelican swallows the fish. A pelican does not use its pouch to store fish. It swallows what it catches right away. A grown pelican can eat 4 pounds (2 kg) of fish every day!

Parrots

There are over 300 kinds of parrots. The smallest is the buff-faced pygmy parrot of New Guinea. It is just over 3 inches (7.5 cm) long. The largest parrot is the hyacinth macaw in South America. It can grow to about 39 inches (1 m) long, although most of its length is its long tail feathers.

The feathers of most parrots are green, but tropical rainforests also have exotic parrots with blue, red, yellow, purple, black, or white feathers. A parrot's strong curved beak and thick tongue help it eat the fruits, nuts, and seeds it gathers. Some parrots also use their beaks as a third foot when they climb trees. Because parrots have such short legs, they can climb better than they can walk.

Name ______________________

Questions About *Beaks and Feathers*

1. What six characteristics do all species of birds have in common?

2. What is *molting*? Why do birds molt?

3. What is unusual about an owl's head? Why is this feature important?

4. Why are most flamingos pink?

5. After catching a fish, what does a pelican have to do before it can fly?

6. In what unusual way do some parrots use their beaks?

Name ________________________________

Vocabulary

A. Look for clues in the text to help you understand the meaning of each word below. Write each word on the line next to its meaning.

vertebrates	molt	species	raptors
sieve	exotic	plumage	talons

1. ______________________ feathers
2. ______________________ the sharp-clawed toes on the feet of some birds
3. ______________________ a group of living things with the same characteristics
4. ______________________ strikingly uncommon
5. ______________________ animals that have an internal skeleton
6. ______________________ to shed and regrow hair or feathers
7. ______________________ birds of prey
8. ______________________ a device with tiny holes that is used for straining liquids

B. The word **adapted** means "changed or adjusted to be suitable for a particular condition or purpose."

Describe one way in which each species below is adapted to its habitat or way of living.

owl ____

flamingo ____

pelican ____

parrot ____

Name ____________________

Possessive Nouns

Possessive nouns can be singular or plural. Notice that when a plural noun ends with **s**, the possessive is formed by adding just an apostrophe.

Examples: A **bird's** wings are covered with feathers. *(singular)*
The structure of **birds'** wings makes birds able to fly. *(plural)*

1. Write **'s** or **s'** on each line to form the singular or plural possessive noun.

   a. The basketball game was held in the school______ gym.

   b. Penguin______ wings are too small for flying.

   c. That woman______ hat is blocking my view of the parade.

   d. You'll find the halters hanging next to the horse______ stalls.

   e. The player______ mitts were lying on the bench.

   f. Sara polished her brother______ football trophy.

2. Find eight possessive nouns in the story and write them on the lines below.

   ____________ ____________ ____________

   ____________ ____________ ____________

   ____________ ____________

3. Which possessive noun in the list above is plural? ____________

4. Pick two singular possessive nouns from the list above and use the plural form of each one in a sentence.

   ____

   ____

   ____

   ____

Name ______________________________

Summarizing

1. Write a one-sentence summary to tell what the first paragraph of the story is about.

2. Write a one-sentence summary to tell what the second and third paragraphs are about.

3. Write a one-sentence summary to tell why birds eat many different kinds of foods.

Think About It

Which bird in the story is your favorite? Explain why you chose this bird and summarize what the story says about the bird.

Out of Space

Ten years had passed since we had blasted off Worim. All the planets in our star system were so crowded that we couldn't find a place to land. I had wanted to stay on Worim and do the best we could, but my folks wouldn't hear of it.

"The worms have eaten everything green and most things that aren't," Mom had said. "We could be next."

"It's now or never," Dad had told me. "Who would have thought that those cute little pet worms everyone had would take over the planet?"

"What if we don't find a new place?" I had asked him.

"Then we'll just take in the scenery until we come to another star system that isn't plagued with worms," Dad had answered.

By now, I was bored watching asteroids, moons, planets, and even the space junk whizzing by. I had seen it all before, year after year—broken-down spaceships, out-of-order satellites, and out-of-business fast-food stations. People just threw them out when they weren't useful anymore, instead of disposing of them properly in a black hole.

There was so much junk in space that the intergalactic TV programs we tried to watch came in garbled. I had watched some great programs transmitted from a place called Earth a while back. Most of the creatures on the programs were unusual looking, but a few looked just like us!

Mom says that I watch too much TV anyway, but I don't know what else she thinks I should do. We ran out of books to read, and we haven't seen a library for five years. Our communication system doesn't work well anymore either. Sometimes, we hear strange voices over our signals. One time, someone was talking about shooting baskets, and I couldn't figure out why anyone would want to hurt a basket. I told Dad he had better be careful where we landed because there could be something a lot worse than worms on some of the planets.

At one point, Mom suggested I do something useful in the garden or in the science lab. I worked in the garden for a year or two, but we just grew the same old food all the time. Working in the garden got so boring that I made a robot in the science lab and designed it to take care of the garden. Every now and then, Dad anchored our transporter to some space junk so we could take a spacewalk. Sometimes, I took off my gravity suit and went air swimming. I floated around and did all sorts of stunts, but even that got boring after a couple of years.

Early this morning, we hitched a ride on some light beams from stars. The transporter was really speeding along until, suddenly, Dad steered us off the beam.

"Look at this!" he said.

Mom and I peered through the monitor. It was another star system. We circled the first planet we came to. It looked deserted. Then Dad set the antigravity button and turned on the search beams, and we went in for a better look. The planet was too small and too cold, so we traveled on without getting out of the transporter.

Mom traded places with Dad and took over the driving so he could have a turn at the monitor. Some of the planets we saw were nothing but gas and noxious fumes, and we didn't see anything to eat on any of them. All of a sudden, there were flying bits of matter everywhere. We were in a meteor storm!

"Look out!" said Mom. "Take cover!"

Mom was a great driver. She miniaturized our ship to get us safely through the storm. When everything was back to normal, we resumed our flight at regular size. By that time, we were in another star system and close to another planet.

We hadn't seen a planet like this since we left our own star system. There were clouds swirling over the planet and signs of water, green spaces, and deserts, everything a Worim needs. Mom steered in close, and Dad turned on the testing equipment.

“It’s a possibility,” Dad said, “but it seems heavily populated.”

We circled the planet a few times, looking for a place to land. The cities had a lot of smoke around them.

“No Worim could survive there,” Dad said. Finally, he pointed at the screen. “Right here!” he shouted. “We can land right here.”

We floated down to a green area and parked the transporter under the biggest plant I had ever seen.

“It’s time to mingle and see what kinds of creatures are here,” Mom said.

The strange beings we saw stared at us, and a few ran off. I asked one for directions to a library, but the creature ran away without speaking.

Dad shook his head and said, “A little rude, I’d say. They could use some Worim etiquette.”

We came to a huge building with the word “Museum” on the front of it. When we walked inside, we immediately saw the skeleton of a giant Maiasaura and thought that we might have to leave this planet quickly.

“It looks a little like my Aunt Worima,” said Mom, “only a lot bigger!”

“Poor fellow,” Dad said. “There must have been some gigantic worms here to do something like this.”

We walked past several more skeletons and looked at the charts and murals on the walls.

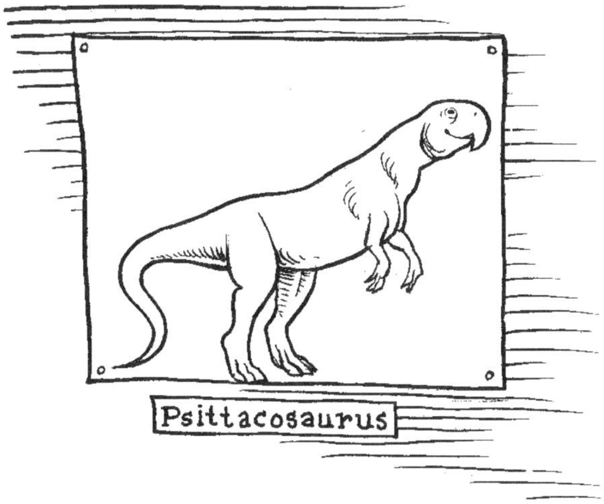

“Look at that!” I said, noticing a picture with a sign below it that said *Psittacosaurus*. “There must be others here just like us!”

“That’s us,” Dad agreed.

We were feeling a little better until we saw creatures with nets running toward us.

“Get ’em!” said one of the creatures.

We pulled ourselves upright and almost flew out the door. We didn’t stop running until we were back inside the transporter and on our way into space.

Name ______________________________

Questions About *Out of Space*

1. What caused the Worims to leave their planet?

2. Why didn't the Worims go to another planet in their star system?

3. What did the narrator believe space creatures should do with broken-down spaceships, out-of-order satellites, and out-of-business fast-food stations?

4. List four activities that the narrator found to do on the space transporter.

5. How did you know that the narrator liked to read?

6. Where do you think the Worims landed? Explain your answer.

7. Why did the Worims leave the new planet?

Name ____________________

Vocabulary

Use the words in the list to complete the sentences below.

blasted	plagued	disposing	system
etiquette	garbled	mingle	transmitted
noxious	deserted	hitched	resumed

1. ____________________ fumes were coming from the chemist's laboratory.
   (poisonous)
2. Crop-destroying insects had ____________________ farmers for years.
   (tormented)
3. When you host a party, you should ____________________ with your guests.
   (mix)
4. Speaking politely to others shows good ____________________.
   (manners)
5. While everyone was at the big game, the town looked ____________________.
   (empty)
6. The pioneers ____________________ teams of oxen to their covered wagons.
   (connected)
7. You can help the environment by ____________________ of trash properly.
   (discarding)
8. The sound from a radio or television becomes ____________________ when a storm interferes with the audio signal.
   (distorted)
9. It took a truckload of dynamite, but the workers finally ____________________ through the solid rock to tunnel under the mountain.
   (exploded)
10. Equipped with a color television camera, the lunar rover ____________________ images of the moon back to Earth.
    (relayed)
11. The ballgame ____________________ after the seventh-inning stretch.
    (continued)
12. The human digestive ____________________ starts at the mouth.
    (configuration)

Name ______________________

Out of Space

Syllables

Write the number of syllables on the line next to each word. Then find the words in the word search puzzle.

noxious	_____	meteor	_____	populated	_____
asteroid	_____	communication	_____	museum	_____
miniaturized	_____	transporter	_____	antigravity	_____
scenery	_____	intergalactic	_____	skeletons	_____
plagued	_____	satellite	_____	monitor	_____

a	l	d	t	r	a	n	s	p	o	r	t	e	r	k	r
c	o	m	m	u	n	i	c	a	t	i	o	n	l	o	t
e	s	x	i	t	a	y	e	d	p	l	n	g	t	i	x
r	k	a	q	c	n	i	n	j	n	o	x	i	o	u	s
s	e	t	i	l	t	o	e	b	z	s	n	n	g	a	d
m	l	t	e	c	i	s	r	m	n	o	l	t	p	i	a
a	e	s	y	k	g	l	y	e	m	e	t	e	o	r	d
u	t	l	m	u	r	o	l	s	g	n	o	r	a	e	u
p	o	p	u	l	a	t	e	d	o	l	e	g	y	s	d
l	n	u	s	a	v	h	t	z	i	t	u	a	r	g	e
a	s	n	e	y	i	c	h	o	s	r	p	l	i	z	m
g	r	a	u	v	t	i	l	a	c	t	i	a	x	u	s
u	t	l	m	g	y	s	a	t	e	x	o	c	n	d	p
e	r	o	i	c	s	a	t	e	l	l	i	t	e	s	a
d	c	a	n	m	i	n	i	a	t	u	r	i	z	e	d
o	r	z	p	e	n	k	s	p	v	r	t	c	d	l	a

Name ______________________

Think About It

1. What clues in the story tell you that the Worims are dinosaur-like creatures?

2. What might have happened to the Worims if they had stayed on the new planet? List three possibilities.

3. Write a new ending to the story, telling what happens when the Worims are captured by the creatures with the nets.

The One-Inch Boy

An Adaptation of a Japanese Folk Tale

In Japan, an old woman and an old man wished for a child to fill their days with happiness. One day, the old man found a basket by his doorway. Tucked snugly in the basket was a child no bigger than the size of a finger. The man called to his wife as he brought the basket into the house.

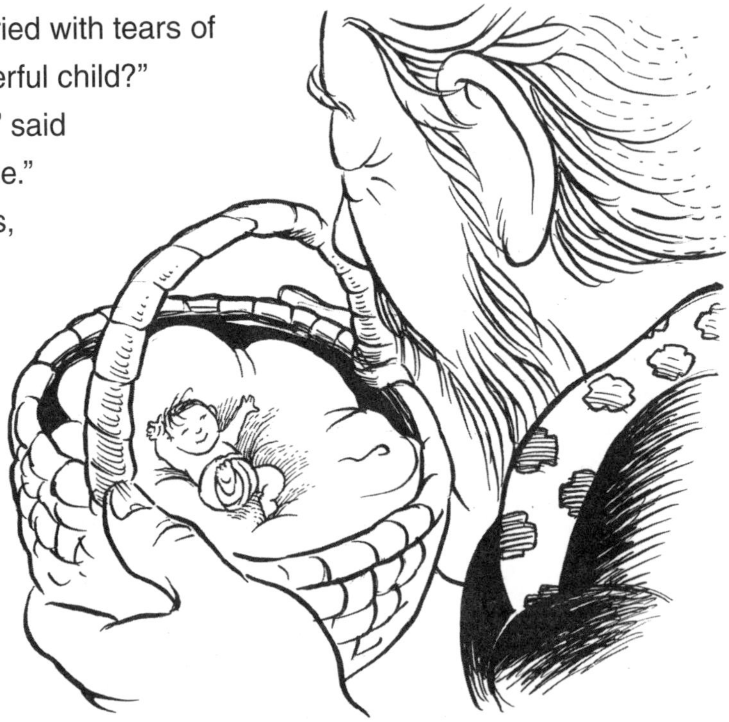

"Oh, husband!" the woman cried with tears of joy. "What shall we call this wonderful child?"

"He is our own one-inch boy," said the man, "and that will be his name."

The old man made tiny chairs, a tiny table, and a tiny bed for his tiny son. The old woman cooked grains of rice for the child to eat and put them in a bowl that the man had carved from wood.

Each day, One-Inch Boy became stronger, but he never grew bigger. Although he was small, One-Inch Boy was very helpful. He crawled under tables and chairs to find things that were lost. He brought in blades of grass that could be dried and woven into mats and shoes. He rode on his father's shoulder through the forest, pointing out fallen limbs that could be gathered for firewood.

Fifteen happy years went by. Then, one day, One-Inch Boy said to his parents, "I want to go to Kyoto to seek my fortune. Will you allow it?"

"But how can we manage without you?" asked his mother.

"Indeed," said his father. "You have given us such great joy."

Although his parents did not want their son to leave, the boy persisted, and they finally agreed. His father found a small lacquer bowl for One-Inch Boy to use as a boat. His mother cut oars from chopsticks and gave him a sewing-needle sword in a straw scabbard. One-Inch Boy set off down the river in the bowl. He had food, his sword, and blessings from his parents, and he promised to send for his parents as soon as he had made his fortune.

All went well during the first days of the journey. Then the weather changed. Tremendous winds and heavy rain tossed the bowl from one side of the river to the other. One-Inch Boy tried to row to shore, but the waves were too high. A boat that was much bigger than the bowl bore down on One-Inch Boy. The waves made by the boat swamped the bowl, and One-Inch Boy was sure he would drown.

"Help! Help!" he called out.

Just when he had given up all hope of being saved, a large hand plucked him out of the water.

"What is this?" the boatman exclaimed. "A boy no bigger than my finger? What are you doing on this dangerous river?"

"I was on my way to Kyoto to seek my fortune," One-Inch Boy responded.

"What a coincidence," said the boatman. "I, too, was on my way to Kyoto to sell a load of wood. Come with me, and we shall go to Kyoto together."

One-Inch Boy was most grateful. The long ride in the bowl had been very tiring. To thank the boatman, One-Inch Boy mended the net bag that the man used to carry the wood.

In Kyoto, he bid the boatman goodbye and set out to see the city. Before long, he came to a beautiful palace. One-Inch Boy easily slipped through the spaces in the iron gate and pounded on the palace doors.

"Noble lord, can you give me shelter while I seek my fortune?" the boy called.

A great man dressed in silk robes opened the doors and looked around.

"I thought I heard someone," he said, "but there is no one."

"Down here, good sir," said One-Inch Boy in his loudest voice. "I will serve you well for food and a place to stay."

The great man picked up One-Inch Boy.

"Well, you have courage, and you ask so little for your services. You may stay here if you wish."

One-Inch Boy thanked the great man, and made himself at home in the beautiful palace. Everyone in the household marveled at the boy's small size, and they gave him all he wished for.

On a spring afternoon, the noble's daughter carried One-Inch Boy on a walk. Her guards and ladies-in-waiting accompanied them. As they passed by a dense forest, an ogre roared from his hiding place behind the trees. Then he grabbed the noble's daughter. Her ladies-in-waiting fled, and so did the guards.

One-Inch Boy spoke crossly to the ogre. "Leave this beautiful lady alone, or you shall feel my sword." One-Inch Boy unsheathed his sword and struck the ogre.

"Not much of a meal," the ogre laughed, "but it will do until I find something else to eat." And, with that, the ogre scooped up One-Inch Boy and swallowed him.

One-Inch Boy stabbed the inside of the ogre's stomach with his sword. The ogre screamed and let go of the noble's daughter, who ran quickly to the palace. One-Inch Boy climbed around inside the ogre, tickling and scratching the beast. When he reached the ogre's mouth, the creature sneezed, and One-Inch Boy flew out. As the wounded ogre whirled around to run back into the forest, he dropped his charmed necklace on the ground. One-Inch Boy picked it up, put it around his neck, and made a wish. Immediately, he was transformed into a tall and handsome nobleman.

In return for saving his daughter, the great lord offered One-Inch Boy half of his lands and his fortune, and the nobleman's daughter happily agreed to marry One-Inch Boy. As he had promised, One-Inch Boy sent for his parents, and they all lived together happily for the rest of their years.

Name ______________________

Questions About *The One-Inch Boy*

1. Despite his tiny size, what things was One-Inch Boy able to do?

2. Name something that One-Inch Boy would not have been able to do.

3. Why did One-Inch Boy want to go to Kyoto?

4. Describe One-Inch Boy's boat and equipment.

5. How did One-Inch Boy's size help him defeat the ogre?

6. What reward did the noble give One-Inch Boy?

7. What promise did One-Inch Boy keep?

Name ______________________________

Vocabulary

A. Write each word below on the line next to its definition.

lacquer	charmed	ogre	journey	scabbard
swamped	persisted	bore	dense	transformed

1. ______________________ enchanted; magical
2. ______________________ a case or holder for the blade of a sword
3. ______________________ thick; packed together
4. ______________________ filled with water; sunk
5. ______________________ a monster in folk tales
6. ______________________ changed
7. ______________________ a long trip
8. ______________________ did not give up
9. ______________________ a highly polished coating on wood
10. ______________________ past tense of "to bear" (to move in the direction of)

B. Write the correct word on the line to complete each sentence.

fortune	tremendous	unsheathed	coincidence	marveled

1. The knight ______________________ his sword as he rode into battle.
2. Our class ______________________ at the enormous dinosaur skeletons on display at the museum.
3. No one really knows what ______________________ life holds for them when they leave home and go out into the world.
4. It's a ______________________ that my best friend and I have the same birthday.
5. A ______________________ snowstorm closed schools and businesses for a week.

Name ________________________________

Sequencing

Number the events in each group below to show the order in which they happened in the story.

Part I

_____ One-Inch Boy traveled down the river in a bowl.

_____ The old man found One-Inch Boy near his doorway.

_____ The bowl was swamped by high waves during a storm.

_____ One-Inch Boy helped his parents.

_____ A boatman rescued One-Inch Boy and took him to Kyoto.

Part 2

_____ The ogre sneezed, and One-Inch Boy was free.

_____ One-Inch Boy asked the great lord for food and shelter.

_____ The ogre swallowed One-Inch Boy.

_____ One-Inch Boy fought inside the ogre.

_____ The ogre grabbed the noble's daughter.

Part 3

_____ One-Inch Boy was transformed into a tall nobleman.

_____ One-Inch Boy sent for his parents.

_____ The noble rewarded One-Inch Boy with half of his lands and fortune.

_____ One-Inch Boy made a wish with the ogre's charmed necklace.

_____ The noble's daughter agreed to marry One-Inch Boy.

Name ______________________

Drawing Conclusions

Read the following paragraph.

> Felicia shuffled up the street toward her house. She could barely put one foot in front of the other. It took enormous effort for her to climb the flight of stairs to her bedroom. Then she collapsed on the bed. A 10-kilometer race was too long.

Although the paragraph does not use the words *tired* or *exhausted,* you know how Felicia feels by the way she is acting. The paragraph does not say exactly why Felicia feels the way she does, but you can tell that she has just run a race. You are able to draw this conclusion based on what you read. A writer does not always explain everything, so readers must often **draw conclusions** by putting information together.

Write a conclusion that you can draw from each of these events in *The One-Inch Boy.*

1. One-Inch Boy's father made a boat for him, and his mother made oars and a sword.

   ____

2. The boatman pulled One-Inch Boy to safety and gave him a ride to Kyoto.

   ____

3. People in the noble's house gave One-Inch Boy whatever he wanted, and the noble's daughter carried him with her on walks.

   ____

4. One-Inch Boy yelled at the ogre and stabbed him in the stomach.

   ____

5. The noble gave One-Inch Boy half of his lands and his daughter's hand in marriage.

   ____

Napkin Rings for Any Occasion

Just think of the occasions when your family sits down to a special meal. There are birthdays, Thanksgiving, Christmas Day, and many more. Wouldn't it be fun to have special napkin rings to decorate the table for each event? They're easy to make. Here's how!

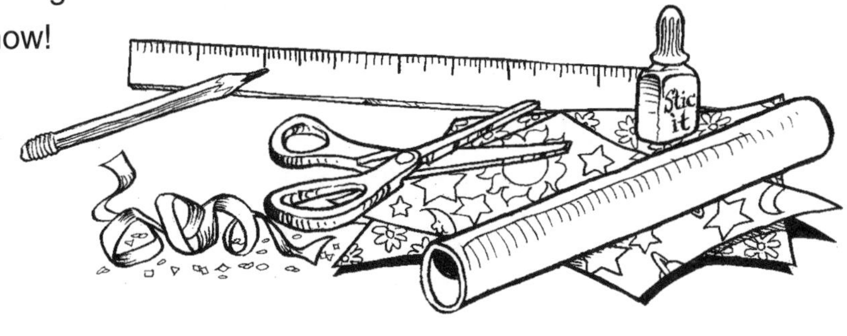

You will need:

- a pen or pencil
- a ruler
- scissors
- glue
- a cardboard tube (from an empty roll of paper towels)
- wrapping paper (or plain paper that you have decorated)
- ribbon, stickers, sequins, glitter, and other decorative items

Directions:

1. Place the ruler along the length of the cardboard tube and make a mark at every inch (2.5 cm).
2. Cut through the tube at each mark to make cardboard rings. Count to see if you have enough rings for everyone. If you need more rings, repeat steps 1 and 2 with another cardboard tube.

3. For each cardboard ring, cut a strip of wrapping paper that measures $5\frac{1}{2}$ inches (14 cm) long and $2\frac{1}{2}$ inches (6.5 cm) wide. If you use plain paper, draw pictures or designs on it before you cut it.
4. Spread glue on the outside of each cardboard ring. (Work with only one ring at a time.)
5. Place the cardboard ring at the center of the strip of paper. Then wrap the paper around the outside of the ring, pressing it firmly onto the glue. (The ends of the paper strip will overlap, and you should have about $\frac{3}{4}$ inch (2 cm) of paper sticking out on each side of the cardboard ring.)

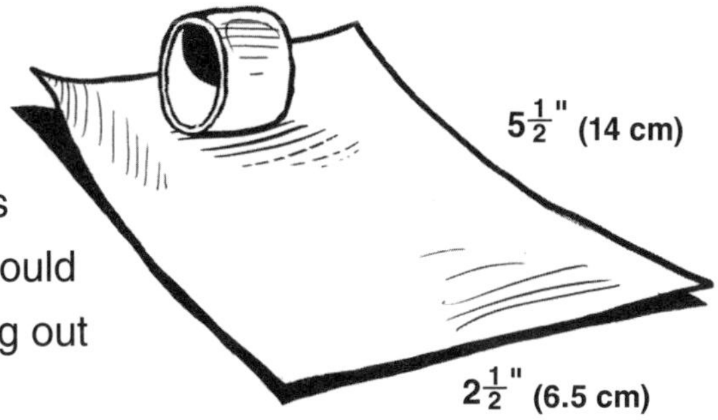

6. Cut into the overhanging paper about every $\frac{1}{2}$ inch (1.25 cm), making paper tabs.

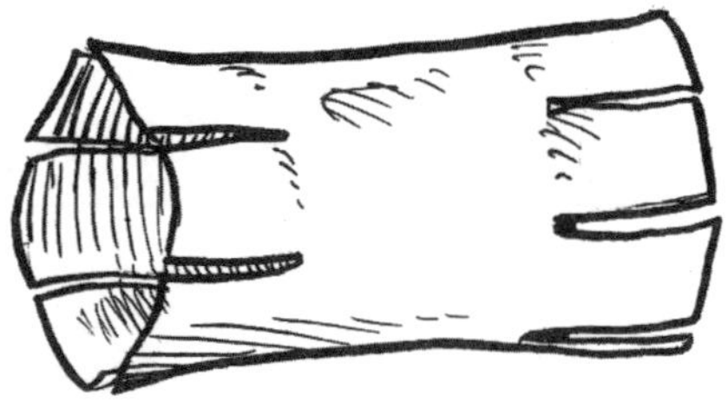

7. Rub glue lightly around both inside edges of the ring. Then fold the paper tabs inside the ring and press them onto the glue.

8. Decorate the outside of the ring with ribbon, stickers, glitter, sequins, or anything else you like.

When a special day comes along, tuck paper or cloth napkins into the decorated napkin rings and put one next to each place setting. You can use napkin rings at special meals any time of the day.

After the event, store the napkin rings in a plastic bag or in a box with a lid. You'll want them to be easy to find for the next holiday or special occasion.

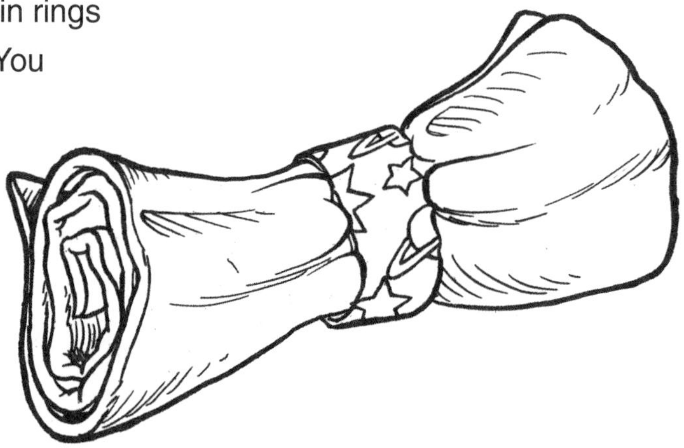

Spread the Fun Around

Invite your friends to make napkin rings with you. Make it a party! You can have all the materials ready for them—and maybe even some punch and cookies. Your work time will be as special as the decorative napkin rings you make.

Keep the Fun Going

Build a collection of napkin rings by making different sets throughout the year. As each holiday or special event approaches, decorate some napkin rings just for that occasion. You can reuse each set when the same event comes around the next year—and every year after that!

Name ____________________

Questions About *Napkin Rings for Any Occasion*

1. What materials do you need to make napkin rings?

2. If you use self-adhesive paper, which item in the list of materials isn't needed? Explain why.

3. How are napkin rings useful?

4. Explain how to use napkin rings.

5. What does the story suggest for making your work time fun?

6. Write an idea of your own for making your work time fun.

Name ____________________

Think About It

1. What is your favorite day of the year to celebrate?

2. Why do you like that day more than any other holiday or celebration?

3. Do you think that homemade decorations make celebrations more special? Explain your answer.

4. What are some of the foods your family prepares and eats on holidays?

5. How could you make your favorite day more fun or more interesting? List ideas for things you and your family could do or make.

Name ____________________

Sequencing

A. Number the directions below in the correct order.

_____ Spread glue around the inside edges of the cardboard ring.

_____ Cut through the tube at each mark.

_____ Fold all of the overhanging paper inside the ring and press it down.

_____ Make cuts in the overhanging paper on each side of the ring.

_____ Place a ruler along the length of a cardboard tube.

_____ Count the rings.

_____ Make a mark on the tube at every inch.

B. Three steps for making napkin rings are missing in the directions above. Write the missing steps in the correct order on the lines below.

1. ____________________

____

2. ____________________

____

3. ____________________

____

C. Write two final steps for making a napkin ring.

1. ____________________

____

2. ____________________

____

Name ______________________________

Writing Directions

Place mats and place cards are two other table decorations that you could make for special occasions or celebrations. Choose one of these decorations and explain how to make it below. Start by writing a list of the materials you will need for the project.

Project *(check one)*: ☐ **Place Mats**

☐ **Place Cards**

You will need: ______________________ ______________________

______________________ ______________________

______________________ ______________________

______________________ ______________________

Directions *(number each step)*:

____

____

____

____

____

____

____

____

____

____

____

The Contest

It all began when a magician proclaimed that the wisest person in the land should be the next governor. The magician also proclaimed that he was the wisest person in the land. No one cared to argue with the magician. He might turn you into a pig or a flowerpot if he wished. It was fearfully agreed, then, that the magician would be the governor. There was nothing else to be said about it. Nothing, that is, until the milkmaid spoke to the laundress.

"The magician is a fraud," the milkmaid said. "He can't turn a frog into a prince or even a caterpillar into a butterfly. And as for being wise, I dare say that my cow is smarter. The magician loses his spectacles when they're right there on his nose. He can't even remember to put on his shoes before he goes outside."

Now, this information would have gone no further than the milkmaid and the laundress if it hadn't been for the shoemaker. He overheard the whole conversation.

"Did you hear what the milkmaid said this morning?" he asked the blacksmith. "The milkmaid," continued the shoemaker, "said that the magician will change us all into frogs if he becomes the governor. Furthermore, she said that he is not even as smart as her cow."

The innkeeper and his wife stopped to exchange greetings as they passed by the blacksmith's shop that afternoon.

"Did you hear what the milkmaid said this morning?" the blacksmith asked them.

The innkeeper and his wife had been busy preparing breakfast for travelers all morning. It upset them to find out now that there was news they didn't know about. They prided themselves on knowing everything. When the villagers wanted to hear the latest gossip, they stopped at the inn for a bowl of hot soup. If the innkeeper and his wife had no real gossip to report, they would make up something.

"Well," continued the blacksmith, "the milkmaid said that the magician was a frog. She also said that she was smarter than he was."

With his pounding and clanging all day, the blacksmith seldom heard anything the way it was said.

Before the day had ended, everyone in the village knew that the milkmaid had challenged the magician to a contest to see which of them was smarter. The winner of the contest would be the next governor. The village teacher, the carpenter, and the seamstress would judge the contest.

The magician was very angry about having to compete with a milkmaid, but he accepted the conditions. His ambition to become governor was strong. The good-natured milkmaid was surprised to learn that she was a candidate for governor. But if the people wanted her wisdom, who was she to say that she wouldn't share it?

On Wednesday, when the sun was directly overhead, all the people from the village and the surrounding countryside gathered at the square. The judges took their places, and the magician stood barefoot in front of them. The milkmaid waved to the crowd as she rode into the square on a cow. Hopping down off the cow, she bowed to the judges.

The first questions that the people asked were simple ones. How many legs does an octopus have? What is your mother's name? Then a farmer said, "Magician, I've always wondered where the center of the earth is."

"Well, it would seem to me..." the magician started. Then he stopped and thumbed through his notebooks. Finally, he said, "I think it must be in the middle of the sea or somewhere."

The milkmaid smiled. "Without a doubt," she said, "the center of the earth is right here under the magician's bare feet."

"Preposterous!" screamed the magician.

"If you doubt me, dear Magician," said the milkmaid, "take a string and measure around the earth from where you stand. If your feet are not right on the center of the earth, if they are even an inch off, then you will win the contest."

The magician knew, of course, that he could not do what the milkmaid suggested, so he could not prove her right or wrong. All he could do was wait for the next question.

"I would like to ask," said the baker, "how many stars are in the sky?"

"How should I, or anyone else, know that?" the magician snapped. "Taking an educated guess, I would say twenty-seven, give or take one or two."

"You're wrong again, Magician," said the milkmaid. "There are as many stars in the sky as there are hairs in your beard. I will pull the hairs out one at a time and count them while you count the stars. If the number is the same, you will know that I am right."

The magician screamed as the milkmaid pulled one hair after another from his beard. Even if the contest had been at night, the magician couldn't count stars while the milkmaid was pulling his beard apart.

"Stop! Stop!" the magician yelled.

"I shall stop when you agree that my answer is correct," said the milkmaid.

"I agree! I agree!" said the magician.

Then, a small child asked, "How do you measure all the water in the sea?"

"It's very easy to do," said the milkmaid. "Just ask the magician to stop all the water in the rivers from flowing into the sea. Then you count the number of milk pails you can fill with seawater."

"I can't do that!" shouted the magician. "How absurd!"

"Do you have a better answer?" asked the milkmaid.

"Of course not," the magician argued. "No one does."

"Then," said the milkmaid, "let the judges choose the next governor."

In minutes, the milkmaid was robed and seated on the governor's chair. The magician was so angry that he began jumping up and down, screaming and stamping his feet. Then, for the first time, he did a magic trick that worked. He turned himself into a toad!

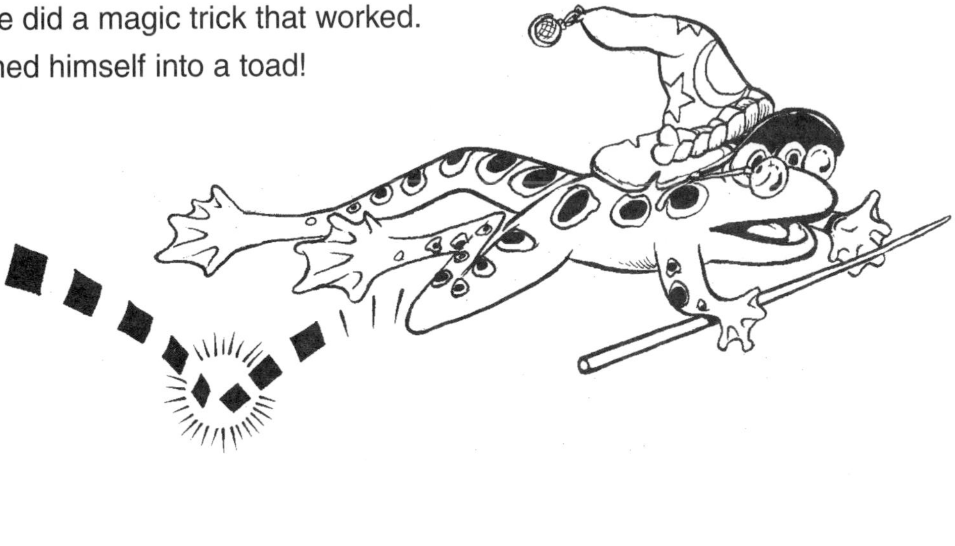

Name ______________________________

Questions About *The Contest*

1. Why did the magician think that he should be governor?

____

2. Why didn't anyone disagree with the magician?

____

____

3. Why did the milkmaid think that the magician was a fraud?

____

____

4. What happened to the conversation between the milkmaid and the laundress as it was passed on from person to person and told over and over? What was the end result?

____

____

____

5. Why did the milkmaid agree to the contest?

____

____

6. What statement did the milkmaid make about the magician at the beginning of the story that proved to be true later on?

____

____

Name ______________________

Vocabulary

Write each occupation mentioned in the story on the line next to its description. Then answer the questions about the occupations.

farmer	milkmaid	blacksmith	magician	teacher	innkeeper
seamstress	governor	laundress	baker	shoemaker	carpenter

1. ______________________ a person in charge of an area and its people
2. ______________________ a person who does magic tricks
3. ______________________ a person who makes and mends footwear
4. ______________________ a person who makes horseshoes and shoes horses
5. ______________________ a person who provides travelers with food and a place to sleep
6. ______________________ a female who milks cows or works in a dairy
7. ______________________ a person who makes bread and pastries
8. ______________________ a female who sews clothing
9. ______________________ a person who helps students learn
10. ______________________ a person who plants, cares for, and harvests crops
11. ______________________ a person who works with wood
12. ______________________ a female who washes clothes

Which occupations are compound words?

____

Name the occupations of the two characters who competed in the contest.

______________________ ______________________

Name the occupations of the three characters who judged the contest.

______________________ ______________________ ______________________

Name ______________________________

Synonyms

Use the words in the word box to complete the crossword puzzle.

Word Box

absurd
argue
candidate
challenged
contest
conversation
fraud
gossip
governor
judges
preposterous
wisdom

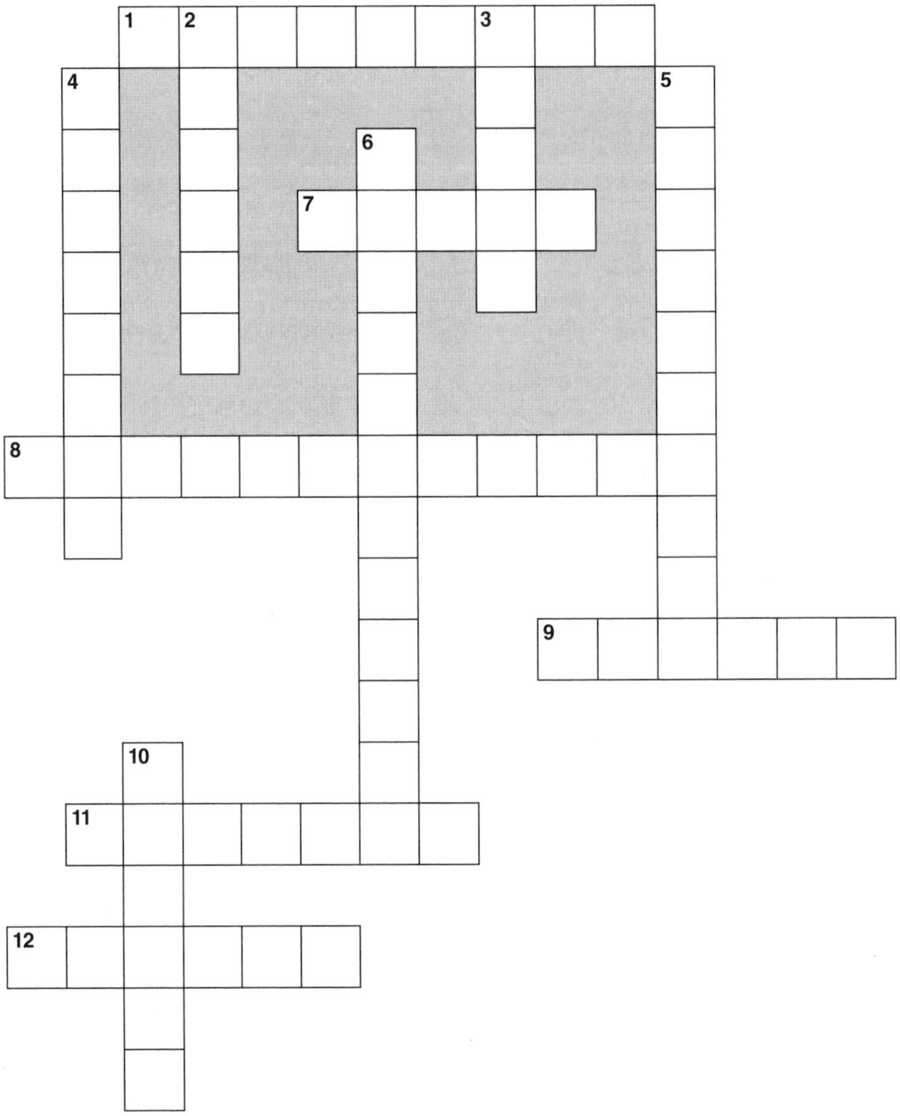

Across

1. nominee
7. imposter
8. chat
9. referees
11. competition
12. intelligence

Down

2. foolish
3. debate
4. ruler
5. dared
6. ridiculous
10. rumors

Name ____________________

Comparing Characters

Write words or phrases that describe the magician, the milkmaid, or both in the appropriate sections of the Venn diagram. Then answer the question below.

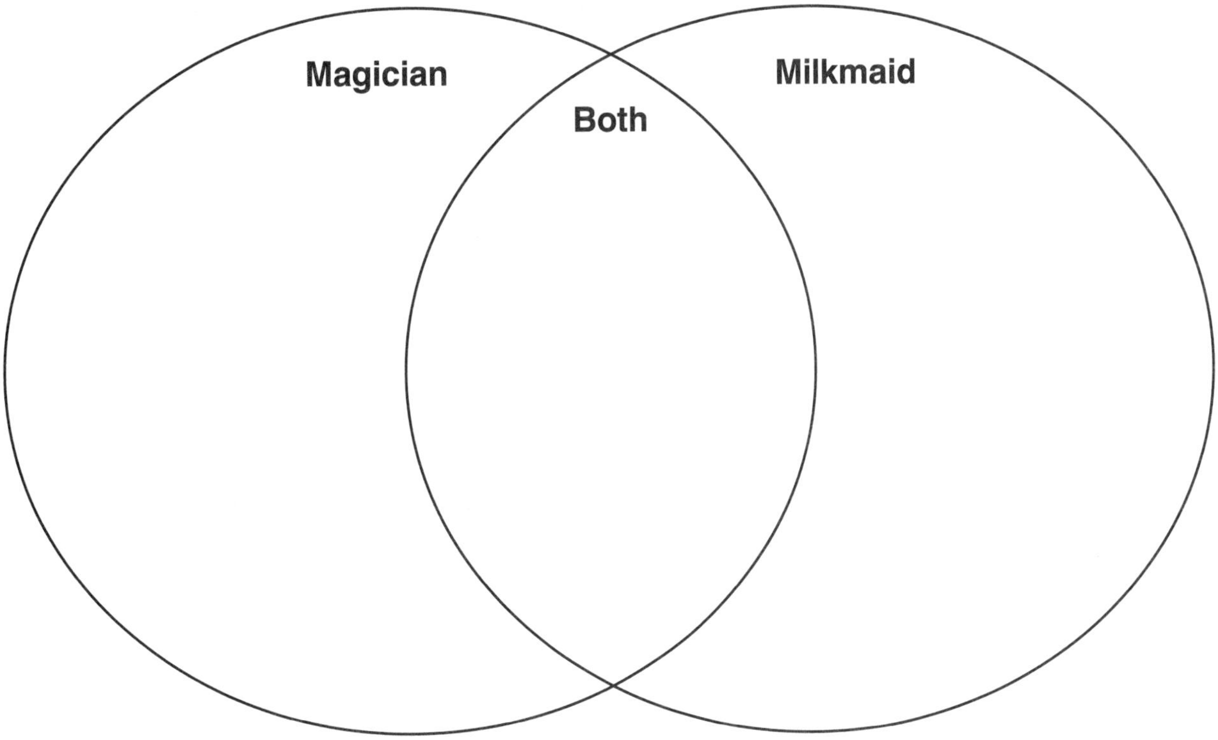

Do you think that the magician or the milkmaid should have been made governor? Explain your answer. Include information from the Venn diagram in your explanation.

____

____

____

____

____

____

____

____

Where in the World?

We're off on a mystery vacation. Use the clues in the story and the map at the end to name our destination.

We're heading south. Pack your beach towel, swimsuit, sun hat, skis, and snow gear. And don't forget the sunscreen! We'll build sand castles, check out a few belching volcanoes, and admire the snow-covered Andes Mountains. There's a very dry desert to cross. In some areas, rain never falls. We'll stop at a green oasis where warm springs supply water for plants and animals. Then we can take a side trip to an island that has mysterious stone statues. Weather permitting, we'll cross icy waters to visit the land of the penguins. We'll have to watch out for icebergs!

Our boat will first dock at Arica, where we'll spend a day or two at the beach. The ocean currents keep the temperature in this coastal city about the same all year. The weather on this wintry August day will be about the same as it would be on a summer day in December.

The country we're visiting is very skinny. We can leave the beach on the western coast in the morning and arrive at a mountain resort near the eastern border in time to enjoy lunch. So there's no hurry. We have plenty of time to take a detour.

Instead of going skiing today, we can travel about 100 miles (160 kilometers) northeast to Parque Lauca. We'll drive from sea level to an altitude of about 13,000 feet (4,000 meters). With our field glasses, we can spot giant condors flying overhead, see vicuña grazing on mountainsides, and track bounding long-eared rabbits. Lago Chungará, one of the highest lakes in the world, is a perfect place to watch flamingos and enjoy a picnic lunch.

When we leave the park, we'll travel south to photograph herds of vicuña in neighboring parks. Let's make sure we have our swimsuits so we can soak in one of the area's thermal hot springs. Farther south, we'll have a close view of the smoking volcano, Guallatiri. Along the road, we'll see flocks of nandu.

Next, we'll drive southwest to Antofagasta, a port on the Pacific Ocean. From there, we'll take a plane to Santiago, the capital city. We won't have much time, however, to tour the old Spanish-style churches and buildings in the city. Our bus leaves early the next morning for a skiing trip in the nearby mountains. After two days of fun in the powdery snow, we'll travel to Valparaíso, where a ship will take us on an ocean voyage to Easter Island.

One of the best ways to travel around Easter Island is on horseback. It's very hot on the island, but wearing a big straw hat will help you stay cool. And keep the camera handy! You'll want to snap pictures of the giant stone statues. They are 18 to 22 feet (5 to 7 m) tall. There are many legends about the people who carved the statues, but just who they were is a real mystery.

When we return to Valparaíso, we'll rest for a day at the beach resort Viña del Mar. Then we'll go on to Puerto Montt, which is a good starting point for exploring the mountain lakes and volcanoes of the southern Andes. On our way to Puerto Montt, we can make time for a river-rafting adventure.

After we hike around the lakes, we'll fly on to Punta Arenas at the southern end of the country. This city is on the Strait of Magellan. It might rain here, so carry your umbrella when you go walking around. If it's a clear afternoon, there will be a breathtaking view from the Cerro del Cruz. Snapping a picture of the view will give us the perfect souvenir of this South American city.

The next day, a cruise ship will take us to Antarctica, where we can see a penguin rookery. It's the last stop on our visit to our southern neighbors. Adiós!

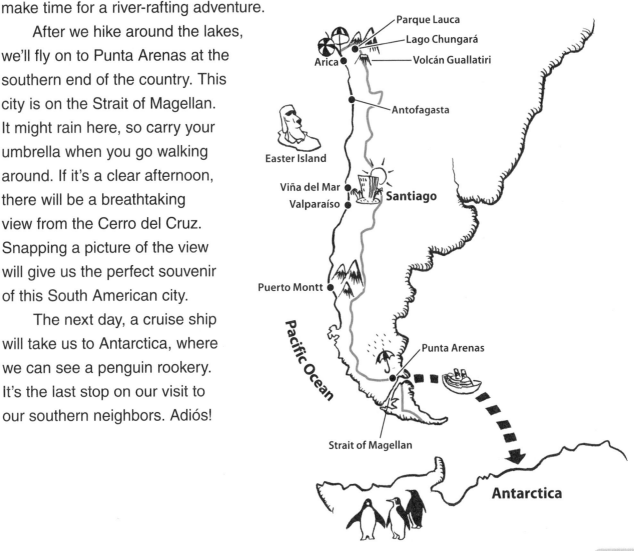

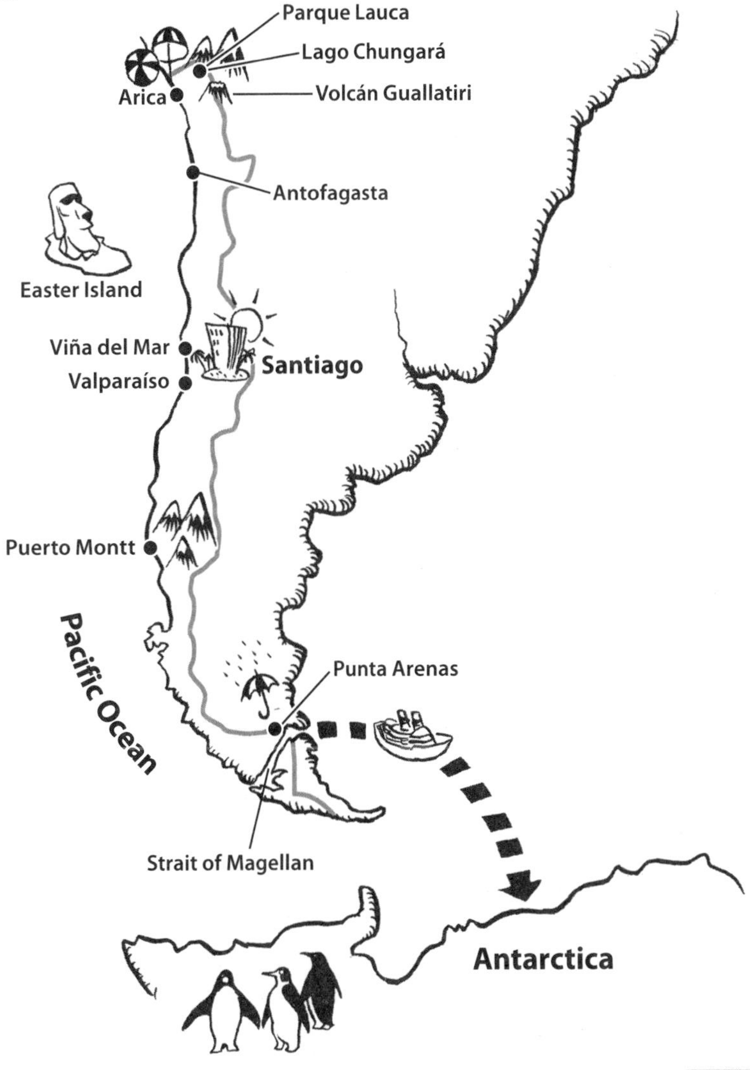

Name ______________________________

Questions About *Where in the World?*

1. What country did you "visit" in the story?

____

2. What are some of the clues in the story that helped you guess the name of the country? List at least five of them.

____

____

____

____

____

3. If you went to this country, which of the activities in the story would you enjoy the most? Explain why.

____

____

____

____

4. What are the natural eastern and western boundaries of this long, narrow country?

____

____

5. Why would you need to take different types of clothing to visit this country?

____

____

____

Name ______________________________

Vocabulary

Write the letter for each word on the line next to its definition.

a. legend	_____ the distance above sea level
b. rookery	_____ an item kept as a reminder of a place visited
c. altitude	_____ capable of producing or holding in heat
d. destination	_____ a strip of water between two larger bodies of water
e. resort	_____ the end or final point of a journey
f. souvenir	_____ an indirect route to a destination
g. strait	_____ a place that offers vacationers lodging and recreation
h. detour	_____ a place where a group of birds nests and breeds
i. currents	_____ an old story that explains the existence of something in nature
j. thermal	
	_____ the movements or flow of water in an ocean, lake, river, or stream

Compound Words

Find nine compound words in the story and write them on the lines below.

______________ ______________ ______________

______________ ______________ ______________

______________ ______________ ______________

Choose one of the compound words above and write sentences using the two words in that compound. Then write a third sentence using the compound word.

____

____

____

Name ______________________________

Sequence the Cities

Write numbers on the lines to show the order in which each location was visited in the story.

_____ Valparaíso

_____ Antofagasta

_____ Antarctica

_____ Parque Lauca

_____ Santiago

_____ Cerro del Cruz

_____ Viña del Mar

_____ Arica

_____ Puerto Montt

_____ Strait of Magellan

_____ Lago Chungará

_____ Easter Island

_____ Punta Arenas

_____ Guallatiri

Reading a Map

Look at the map on page 79 to answer the following questions.

1. Which cities or points of interest in the list above are located along the Pacific Coast?

____

____

2. Write the name of the country's capital city and describe its location.

____

3. Which direction would you have to travel to go from Viña del Mar to Easter Island?

   Ⓐ north Ⓑ northwest Ⓒ northeast

4. Which direction would you have to travel to go from Punta Arenas to Antarctica?

   Ⓐ north Ⓑ northwest Ⓒ south

Name ____________________

Write About It

Use what you learned about the country in the story to design a travel poster or an advertisement inviting tourists to visit there.

A Biography of John Muir

1838–1914

John Muir was born in Scotland. In February 1849, ten-year-old John sailed with his father, a brother, and a sister across the Atlantic Ocean to America. John's father had heard that there was good farmland in a new state called Wisconsin.

When they reached America, the Muirs took a boat up the Hudson River to Albany, New York. Continuing by boat, they traveled west to Buffalo on the Erie Canal. From there, they went on to Milwaukee through the Great Lakes. And still their travels had not ended. From Milwaukee, they traveled 100 miles (161 kilometers) by horse and wagon into the Wisconsin wilderness. They cleared 80 acres near the Fox River to plant corn and wheat.

That November, the rest of the Muir family arrived in Wisconsin. John and his brothers and sisters plowed, chopped weeds, hoed, and cut crops by hand. They worked so hard that their health suffered. John's father was very strict and did not allow the children to take any breaks during the day.

John worked hard, but he also managed to keep track of the many different birds he saw. He studied the wildflowers in the area, too, whenever he could.

After the land was worn out from the many crops they had planted, the Muir family moved 6 miles (10 km) away and started a new farm.

John had wanted time to read, but his father thought that books were worthless. He wouldn't even allow John to stay up late with his books. He told John to get up earlier in the morning if he wanted to read.

In Wisconsin, it was often too cold to read in the early morning, so John would go to the cellar to work on inventions instead. One of his inventions was an early-rising machine. The device kept track of hours, days of the week, and months. John had whittled all the parts from wood. When it was time for him to get up, a rod tipped his bed upright, and John greeted the day standing up.

In 1860, at age twenty-two, Muir took his inventions to a fair in Madison, Wisconsin. Some of the inventions won prizes, and his exhibit led to a job in a machine shop. It also led to classes at the University of Wisconsin.

Muir worked on farms in the summer and taught school in the winter so he could afford to take classes when he had time.

John Muir was interested in all kinds of things. His interest in botany prompted him to travel to Canada to study the plants that grew there. When he returned to the United States, he went to work in a sawmill in Indianapolis, Indiana. The owners of the mill gave him time to study plants. In his spare time, Muir also invented better ways to make wooden tools.

One evening at work, a piece of metal flew into Muir's eye. For a time, he couldn't see out of that eye. Then the other eye became temporarily blind, too. When Muir's sight returned, he left Indiana and walked 1,000 miles (1,609 km) to the Gulf of Mexico. All along the way, he learned more about people, nature, and plants. Then he took a boat to California.

Muir arrived in California in 1868 and went to Yosemite Valley. There, he worked as a sheepherder and in a sawmill. He also hiked and climbed mountains, studying glaciers and plants. Soon, he started to write about nature. His writing appeared in both magazines and newspapers. People all over the world read Muir's stories, and tourists traveling to California by train wanted to see Muir's Yosemite. Many visitors were well-known politicians and writers.

In 1889, Robert Underwood Johnson, the editor of *The Century Magazine,* came to see the wildflowers in Yosemite. When Muir explained that sheep had grazed them away, the two men joined forces to save Yosemite. Muir wrote articles, and Johnson went to Washington, D.C., to convince important people in the government to make Yosemite a national park.

In 1890, Congress passed a law creating Yosemite National Park. In 1891, President Benjamin Harrison set aside more land in the western states for national forests. After a camping trip in Yosemite with Muir, President Theodore Roosevelt preserved millions of acres in the west for forests and parks.

Muir's writings about plants and nature made people realize that saving America's forest and wildlife areas was important. His books *The Mountains of California* (1894) and *Our National Parks* (1901) were very popular.

In 1892, Muir cofounded the Sierra Club. This organization is dedicated to the protection of land, trees, plants, and water. The Sierra Club still exists today and has many enthusiastic supporters.

John Muir died on December 24, 1914. A stand of giant redwood trees in California was named Muir Woods to honor his efforts to preserve America's natural resources.

Muir is also commemorated on the California state quarter, issued in 2005 by the United States Mint as part of its 50 State Quarters Program.

Name ____________________

Questions About *A Biography of John Muir*

1. How could you tell that learning was very important to John Muir?

2. Describe Muir's early-rising machine.

3. List five different kinds of work that John Muir did during his lifetime.

4. What was Muir's role in saving Yosemite?

5. Do you think that John Muir was a good writer? Explain why or why not.

6. Do you think that preserving natural areas in our country is important? Explain why or why not.

Name ______________________________

Vocabulary

A. Write the letter of the correct definition on the line in front of each word.

______ commemorate	a. started or established an organization along with one or more other people
______ temporarily	b. the study of plants
______ whittle	c. to honor the memory of
______ botany	d. a slow-moving mass of ice
______ exhibit	e. a group of people who join together for a specific purpose or activity
______ glacier	f. an underground room or area below a house
______ cellar	g. to shape a piece of wood by cutting it with a sharp knife
______ cofounded	h. a show or display of objects
______ politicians	i. for a short period of time
______ organization	j. elected officials

B. Circle the adjectives below that you think describe John Muir.

lazy ingenious studious hardworking concerned adventurous stingy

C. Use the clue below each sentence to help you find the correct word from the story to fill in the blank.

1. National parks and forests are preserved ________________________ areas.
   Clue: Places where plants and animals remain in their natural states

2. Muir Woods is a ________________________ of giant redwood trees in California.
   Clue: A five-letter word that means "a group" or "an area"

3. John Muir worked on his ________________________ very early in the morning.
   Clue: Ideas or devices that offer new ways of doing things

Name ______________________________

Going Places

A. John Muir hiked in and traveled to many different places. Fill in the blanks below with the places mentioned in the story.

1. John Muir was born in the country of ____________________.

2. Muir crossed the ____________________ Ocean with his father, brother, and sister to come to America.

3. The Muirs traveled up the ____________________ River and then continued west on the ____________________ Canal and across the ____________________ Lakes to reach ____________________.

4. Muir's family cleared ground for a farm near the ____________________ River in the state of ____________________.

5. Muir traveled north to the country of ____________________ to study plants.

6. When Muir left ____________________, he walked 1,000 miles (1,609 km) to the Gulf of ____________________ and then took a boat to ____________________, where he worked as a sheepherder and at a sawmill in ____________________ Valley.

B. Write the names of places in the story that belong under the following headings.

Bodies of Water	States
____________________	____________________
____________________	____________________
____________________	____________________
____________________	____________________
____________________	
____________________	

Name ______________________________

Make an Information Map

Write at least two facts in each box.

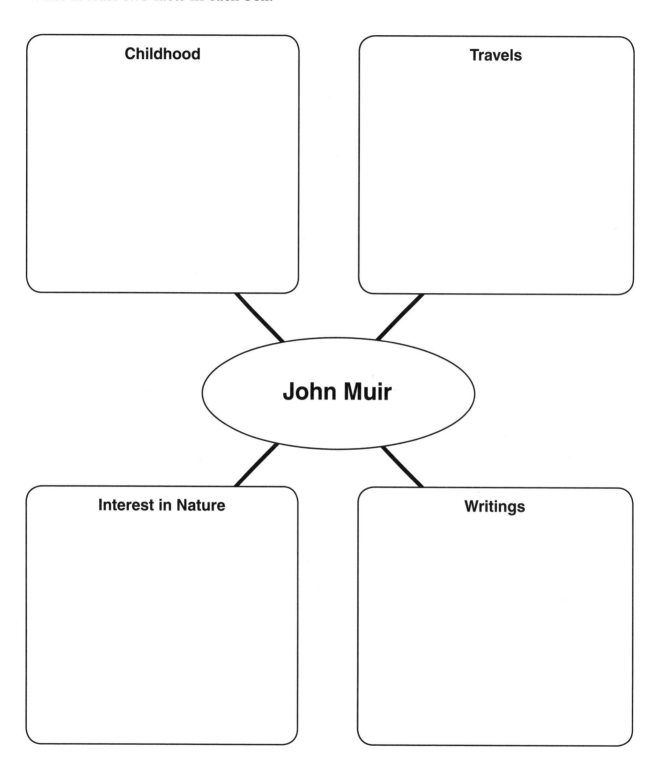

Childhood

Travels

John Muir

Interest in Nature

Writings

Dancing to the Drum

A powwow is a Native American celebration of culture and pride. Powwows are held all year-round throughout the United States. They take place in small towns and large cities. They happen on reservations, in parks, and at fairgrounds. A powwow may go on for several hours or a few days. Sometimes, only a few families gather for a powwow. Other times, thousands of people come together to celebrate. A powwow may be held in honor of a good harvest or a new baby, or it may be just a celebration of life.

The Drum

The Drum is the lifeblood of a powwow. At a powwow, "drum" has two meanings. It is the actual instrument, but it is also the singers and dancers who perform around the instrument. The Drum is positioned at the center of the arena, with the dancers colorfully dressed in beads and feathers, and, sometimes, with their skin painted. Their costumes often have bright and beautiful designs and may include bells, bones, and leather. A dancer's clothing may tell something about his or her tribe's heritage. The drum itself is colorful, too, and usually very large, with a rawhide pad stretched over a painted wooden base that is 3 to 4 feet (1 to 1.25 meters) tall.

Dances and Ceremonies

The Drum performs hours of songs and dances. Custom directs that each song must be different. No song is repeated, even if the powwow lasts three or four days. The Head Man and Lady of the Drum dance first. Then many other powwow participants join in. Some singers and dancers of a Drum travel from powwow to powwow. At each stop, they entertain a whole new crowd.

Many types of dances are performed at a powwow, including traditional dances, grass dances, jingle dress dances, and gourd dances. Some are formal and ceremonial. Others are just for fun. Some of the songs and dances have special rules. When the Drum performs a blanket song, people at the powwow contribute gifts (usually money) before joining in the dance. During a war dance, the dancers are not allowed to take a break unless they all do it together. A give-away ceremony honors a special family. The honored family dances in a circle, while others offer the family gifts and then join in the dance. Finally, the honored family shares a gift with someone they would like to honor.

Contests

Many of the dancers participate in contests. Their costumes are judged, and songs with unusual rhythms and breaks test the dancers' abilities. The number of dances a contestant performs is also considered. There are many levels of competition. If you're old enough to dance, you're old enough to enter a contest. Singers compete, too, and there may also be contests for crafts and games.

Crafts, Games, and Goodies

A crafts fair is often located just outside the arena at a powwow. The fair offers Native American arts and crafts for sale, and elders are usually present to share stories and skills with the younger generations.

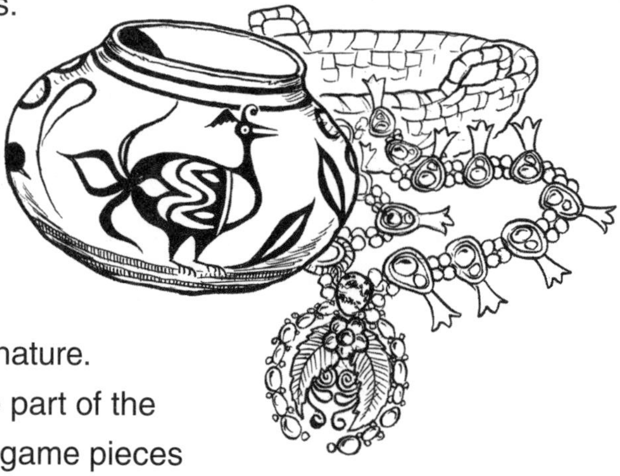

Many of the paintings and jewelry items for sale are made with natural materials such as sand, plant dyes, stones, seeds, and shells. The colors and symbols used in Native American arts and crafts often tell a story. Most of the stories show a deep respect for living things and for the beauty of nature.

Traditional games and foods may also be part of the crafts fair. Many Native American games use game pieces from nature, such as stones and tree limbs. The rules of the games are usually simple, so young children and older adults often play the games together.

Corn and wheat are the main ingredients of many of the foods that are available. Fry bread is perhaps the most popular traditional food. The crisp, flat, deep-fried dough can be served with beans, meat, or cheese for a main meal, but it can also be dessert. Served with honey or powdered sugar, it is usually the children's favorite.

Questions About *Dancing to the Drum*

1. How does a powwow celebrate the pride and culture of Native Americans?

____

____

2. What are some of the events that powwows celebrate?

____

____

3. What is the importance of the Drum at a powwow?

____

____

____

4. Fill in each circle below with words and phrases that indicate what happens in each area of a powwow.

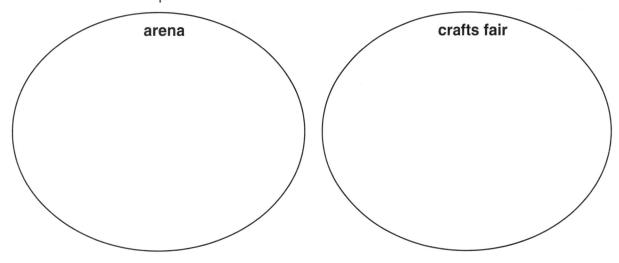

arena

crafts fair

5. Why does Native American art probably include so many symbols that come from nature?

____

____

Name ______________________________

Vocabulary

A. Write the letter of the correct definition on the line in front of each word.

______ arena	a. beliefs and customs passed down through ancestors
______ competition	b. tradition
______ contestant	c. the older people of a family group or community
______ culture	d. an area enclosed for an event
______ custom	e. competitor
______ dyes	f. untanned cowhide
______ elders	g. social background
______ heritage	h. self-respect
______ honor	i. contest
______ lifeblood	j. colorings
______ pride	k. to hold in high regard
______ rawhide	l. the most important feature or element

B. Use the words below to fill in the blanks.

ceremonial   generation   harvest   reservation   respect

1. My Native American friend, Tala, lives on a ______________________ that was given to her tribe by the United States government.
2. A ______________________ fire is kept burning constantly at some Native American powwows.
3. ______________________ festivals celebrate the crops gathered at the end of the growing season.
4. Customs and traditions are passed down from one ______________________ to the next.
5. Native American beliefs include a love of nature and ______________________ for a tribe's elders.

Name ______________________________

Compare Celebrations

1. Compare a Native American powwow to a festival or celebration that you have attended. Tell how the events are alike and how they are different.

2. Would you enjoy attending a powwow? Explain why or why not.

Name ________________________________

Think About It

Answer the questions below to help you think about how you would plan a festival to celebrate your own culture.

1. What would you call your festival?

____

2. What kinds of music, songs, and dances common in your culture would be performed at your festival?

____

____

3. What types of arts and crafts would be displayed or taught at your festival?

____

____

4. What foods or special dishes of your culture would be available at your festival?

____

____

5. Describe the traditional clothing of your culture.

____

____

6. What stories, poems, or folk tales come from your culture?

____

____

Bonus: On a separate sheet of paper, draw a picture of the layout for your festival, showing the activities that will take place and where each one will be located.

The Tower

King Alexander wanted the moon. He was sure that the moon was filled with gold, and he had declared a rule that all gold should belong to the greatest king in the universe. Since he had also declared that he was the greatest king in the universe, he felt entitled to the moon's gold.

"I must add the moon to my royal treasury," he said to his royal advisor.

"Impossible," said the royal advisor. "The moon is far beyond your reach. But if your royal hands can't touch it, neither can anyone else's. The moon's gold is safe where it is."

As the king watched the moon shrink and grow, he reasoned that someone must be able to reach it.

One night, while looking through his telescope at a thin crescent moon, he exclaimed, "Not only has someone reached the moon, but he has also been stealing my gold. It's almost gone! If I can catch the thief, the moon will keep growing bigger and bigger and will never shrink."

Of course, the king didn't stop to think that if a thief was taking gold out of the moon, the same thief, or someone else, was filling it up again.

"Bring me the wisest person in the kingdom," the king commanded his royal advisor. "I need help if I am to reach the moon."

"But, Your Highness," the royal advisor responded, "you have proclaimed *yourself* to be the wisest person in the kingdom."

"Then bring me the second-wisest person," demanded the king.

The royal advisor searched the kingdom. No one would assume the role of the second-wisest person. All the king's subjects knew about the king's royal temper. If they didn't do what he asked, he would toss them into the royal jail.

The royal advisor continued his search until, one day, he saw two goatherds caring for their animals on the slopes of a mountain.

"Good day," the royal advisor called out to the goatherds. "I am looking for the second-wisest person in the kingdom."

"That must be my older brother," said one goatherd, pointing to the other. "He knows where to find the best grasses in the land so that our goats provide the richest milk, which he makes into the finest cheese in the kingdom."

"Wise, indeed," said the royal advisor. "If you come with me, you can help our king with a difficult problem."

"I am happy to help," said the goatherd. "I know everything there is to know about goats."

The goatherd and the royal advisor arrived at the palace and went to the king.

"Your Highness," the royal advisor announced, "this goatherd is the second-wisest person in the kingdom. He will help you reach the moon."

"The moon?" asked the goatherd. "I thought you needed help with goats."

"What would I do with goats?" the king asked. "Since you are the second-wisest person in the kingdom, you must find a way to reach the moon. You have seven days to come up with a plan. If you don't think of something, I will throw both you and the royal advisor in jail forever."

The royal advisor took the confused goatherd to his room, where they spent half the night trying to think of a plan. Finally, they could stay awake no longer. While the goatherd slept, he dreamed that he was back with his goats. They were grazing on a hillside. He dreamed about the fresh apples on the trees that dotted the hillside. He dreamed that he stood on an old barrel to reach the fruit high up in the tree. The next morning, the goatherd told the royal advisor about the dream. Together, they drew a picture of a great tower and marched off to see the king.

"We have the answer, Your Highness," said the royal advisor. "Have the royal tax collector bring every barrel in the kingdom. We'll have the royal carpenter fasten the barrels together into a tower. You can climb to the top of the tower and reach the moon."

The whole kingdom watched the tower grow from the ground, up past the trees, and higher than the castle walls. Every piece of wood in the kingdom, even tables and chairs and beds, was used to make the tower high enough.

"It's high enough," King Alexander said one day. "I'll wait no longer. Today is the day I'll climb to the moon."

"Your Highness," said the advisor, "it's a very long climb. You should send me in your place."

"Since I am the greatest king in the universe and the wisest person in the kingdom," the king answered, "I will have the honor of reaching the moon first. You may climb up later with my dinner."

When the king reached the very top of the tower, he stretched out his arm to touch the moon.

"I must be a little higher," he called out. "Send up another table or chair or box—anything."

"I fear there is nothing left to send up," the royal advisor called back. "Not even a butter churn."

"Then take something off the bottom and throw it up here," the king replied.

"Your Majesty," the goatherd said, "that's impossible. If we take something off the bottom, the tower will..."

"I command you to take something off the bottom!" the king bellowed.

The goatherd looked at the royal advisor. The royal advisor nodded, and the goatherd pulled a barrel from the bottom of the tower.

Name ____________________

Questions About *The Tower*

1. How did the king try to ensure that he would get the gold in the moon?

2. In what ways did the king show his stupidity?

3. Why did the royal advisor try to help the goatherd think of a way to reach the moon?

4. What was the inspiration for the goatherd's plan?

5. Do you think that the goatherd was clever or stupid? What fact or facts in the story support your opinion?

6. Write a final sentence for the story.

Name ______________________________

Vocabulary

Write each word below on the line next to its definition.

crescent	entitled	beyond	impossible	royal
proclaimed	universe	declared	telescope	goatherd
provide	treasury	command	reasoned	assume

1. ______________________ to give what is needed
2. ______________________ cannot be done
3. ______________________ all galaxies and solar systems together
4. ______________________ a person who takes care of goats
5. ______________________ to give an official order
6. ______________________ made a public announcement
7. ______________________ deserving or having a right to something
8. ______________________ a place where money and valuable objects are stored
9. ______________________ a device that helps a person see faraway objects as if they were close
10. ______________________ the term for the shape of the moon when it looks like a backward *C* with pointed ends
11. ______________________ having to do with kings, queens, and their families
12. ______________________ past a particular point
13. ______________________ to take on as a right or a responsibility
14. ______________________ stated with authority
15. ______________________ analyzed or made sense of

Name ______________________________

Problems and Solutions

Identify each of the following phrases as a problem or a solution and write it under that heading for the correct character.

had to come up with a plan	decided to catch the thief
came across two goatherds	needed help to reach the moon
thought gold was being stolen	might get thrown into jail, too
had to find the second-wisest person	helped the goatherd
dreamed about picking fruit	still couldn't reach the moon
sent his advisor to find the second-wisest person	demanded that something be taken from the bottom and added to the top

King Alexander

Problem	Solution
______________________	______________________
______________________	______________________
______________________	______________________

Royal Advisor

Problem	Solution
______________________	______________________
______________________	______________________
______________________	______________________

Goatherd

Problem	Solution
______________________	______________________
______________________	______________________
______________________	______________________

Name ______________________

Write About It

This story is written from the storyteller's point of view. Think about how the story would change if the goatherd was telling it. Write a brief retelling of the story from the goatherd's point of view on the lines below.

Maria Tallchief

Maria Tallchief inherited the proud bearing and grace of the Osage. The famous ballerina was born Elizabeth Marie Tall Chief in 1925. Her father, Alex Tall Chief, was a prominent member of the Osage tribe.

The Tall Chief family lived on the Osage reservation in a big brick house atop the highest hill in Fairfax, Oklahoma. The Osage received a great deal of money when oil was found under their tribal land. Alex Tall Chief's share was more than enough to support his family, so he never felt any need to go to college or to have a career.

Maria's no-nonsense mother came from Irish and Scottish ancestors. Her husband's lack of ambition troubled Ruth Tall Chief. She wanted her two daughters to get more out of life. She also felt that music should be a part of their lives, and she wanted them both to have careers on the stage.

Maria and her younger sister, Marjorie, began lessons in music and dance at about the age of three. Even while they were quite young, both girls showed great promise. When Maria was eight years old, her mother decided that the family should move to California. She felt that Maria and Marjorie would have a better chance in Hollywood.

Maria knew that she wanted to be a dancer or a musician, but she couldn't decide which. Her mother thought that she should be a concert pianist. Although Maria enjoyed playing piano, she disliked the long hours of practicing alone. She liked being with people.

Shortly after the Tall Chief family moved to California, Maria and Marjorie began studying ballet. Their teacher, Bronislava Nijinska, was well-known in the world of dance. She had been a famous ballerina in Russia before opening her own ballet school in the United States.

Madame Nijinska was a wonderful but demanding teacher. She told Maria and Marjorie that they had to start over. She said that they had talent, but they had learned everything wrong. She made Maria work harder than ever, but she also encouraged her and helped her come to a decision. Maria began to see herself as a ballerina.

Maria studied with Madame Nijinska for five years. Then, after finishing high school, she was asked to tour with the Ballet Russe de Monte Carlo, a professional ballet company. For a stage performer, *to tour* means to go from city to city, dancing onstage.

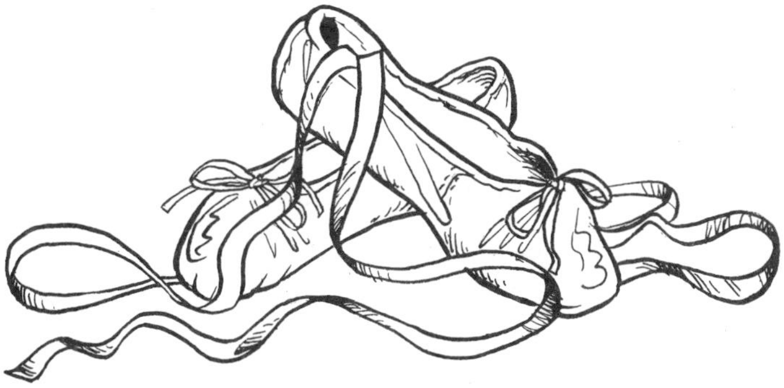

Because Maria was only seventeen, her mother and father were concerned about her traveling without them. Also, Ruth Tall Chief still felt that her daughter should become a concert pianist. Maria, however, was determined to dance, and her parents finally let her accept the job.

Joining the Ballet Russe de Monte Carlo was an exciting new beginning for Elizabeth Marie Tall Chief. It also led her to change her first name to Maria and her last name to one word—Tallchief. Maria worked very hard on the tour. When it ended, she was asked to keep dancing for the company and became one of its star ballerinas.

Then Maria met George Balanchine. Russian-born Balanchine was a leader in American ballet. He was also one of its most creative choreographers. A *choreographer* plans steps for dancers and trains the dancers to do the steps. Most people did not think that American ballet was as beautiful as European and Russian ballet, but Balanchine changed that. The ballets that he created were original and exciting. He also trained dancers to use their strengths, and he showed Maria Tallchief how to become an even better dancer.

In 1946, Maria married Balanchine, and one year later, she joined his ballet company, the New York City Ballet. The company became very popular—and so did Maria. Around the world, people were awed by her talent. Newspapers called her "enchanting," "brilliant," and "electrifying." She became the first world-class prima ballerina in the United States. A *prima ballerina* is a gifted dancer who is featured in ballets as a star performer.

In 1951, Maria's marriage to Balanchine ended, but she stayed with the New York City Ballet. She danced there for many years, performing in as many as eight shows a week. In 1956, Maria married again and, in 1959, had a daughter. In 1965, Maria Tallchief finally retired from the New York City Ballet. She was ready for new challenges.

Maria worked first with the Chicago Lyric Opera Ballet and briefly with the Hamburg Ballet. Then, in 1980, she started her own company, the Chicago City Ballet. There, she and her sister, Marjorie, taught young dancers to love the ballet. In more recent years, Maria has been connected with the Chicago Festival Ballet.

Maria Tallchief was honored in 1996 with a Kennedy Center award for her life's accomplishments in the arts. Among the many other honors she has received, her home state of Oklahoma gave her the name *Wa-Xthe-Thomba,* which means "Woman of Two Worlds." The name celebrates her achievements as both a prima ballerina and a Native American.

Name ________________________________

Questions About *Maria Tallchief*

1. How did each of the people listed below influence Maria Tallchief's life?

   Ruth Tall Chief: ________________________________

   Madame Nijinska: ________________________________

   George Balanchine: ________________________________

2. How did Maria's father, Alex Tall Chief, support his family?

3. What was Maria's full name at birth? When did she change it?

4. With which professional ballet company did Maria become a world-class prima ballerina? How many years did she perform with this company?

Name ______________________________

Vocabulary

A. Write at least six adjectives that describe Maria Tallchief.

______________________________ ______________________________

______________________________ ______________________________

______________________________ ______________________________

B. Use the correct word from the list below to fill in the blank in each sentence.

company	awed	original	strengths	bearing
retired	electrifying	ambition	determined	promise

1. Jaime studied for three hours last night. He's ______________________ to get a good grade on today's science test.
2. Keisha was so exciting in her role as Juliet! She gave an ______________________ performance.
3. We need ______________________ stories for the creative writing contest. Please don't imitate stories by other writers.
4. My grandmother ______________________ from her job last year. Now she and Granddad can spend more time with us.
5. That runner's weakness is that she isn't a fast starter. Her ______________________ are that she is smart and can run a long way without getting tired.
6. Driving along the Pacific coast, we were ______________________ by the brilliant sunset. It painted the entire sky with dazzling shades of pink, orange, and purple.
7. The nobles agreed that the young prince had the regal ______________________ of a king. He showed remarkable strength and self-confidence for a boy of fourteen.
8. The Mainstage Players was the best acting ______________________ in the city. Ali felt honored to be part of such a highly acclaimed theater group.
9. Kyle's dad thought that his son showed great ______________________ as a golfer. He won his first amateur tournament, scoring under par on every hole.
10. Sara loved to be around animals. Her ______________________ was to become a veterinarian, but for now, she was happy just being a volunteer at the animal shelter.

Name ______________________

Compare the Arts

Performing arts involve an artist doing something for an audience. Ballet is an example of a performing art. **Visual arts** involve an artist making something for other people to look at. Painting is an example of a visual art.

1. List three more examples of performing arts and visual arts.

Performing Arts	Visual Arts
______________	______________
______________	______________
______________	______________

2. What visual or performing arts do you enjoy? Tell what you like most about each one.

____

____

____

____

3. Would you rather be the artist or in the audience? Explain your answer.

____

____

4. List three artists you know or admire, describe the art form each one performs, and tell whether that art form is a performing art or a visual art. The artists you list do not have to be famous; they can be family members or friends.

____

____

____

Name ______________________________

Maria Tallchief

Think About It

A. Maria Tallchief enjoyed both piano and ballet. It was a hard decision to choose between them. Do you think she made the right decision? Tell why or why not.

____

____

____

____

B. Think about a choice you have had to make that was a hard decision. Use the T-chart below to show what you had to choose between. Then list the reasons why you might have chosen each of them.

Reasons to ____________________	Reasons to ____________________

Bonus: On another sheet of paper, write a paragraph about the choice you made and how you came to your decision.

Cheng Wan's Visitor

Thirteen-year-old Cheng Wan lives in San Francisco's Chinatown, where his father runs an import business. One warm July Monday, his father's business partner, who lives in Montana, arrived with his ten-year-old son, Danny. While Cheng's father discussed business with his partner, Cheng gave Danny a tour of Chinatown. That night, Cheng wrote a timeline in his diary telling how he spent the day with Danny.

9:00 a.m.

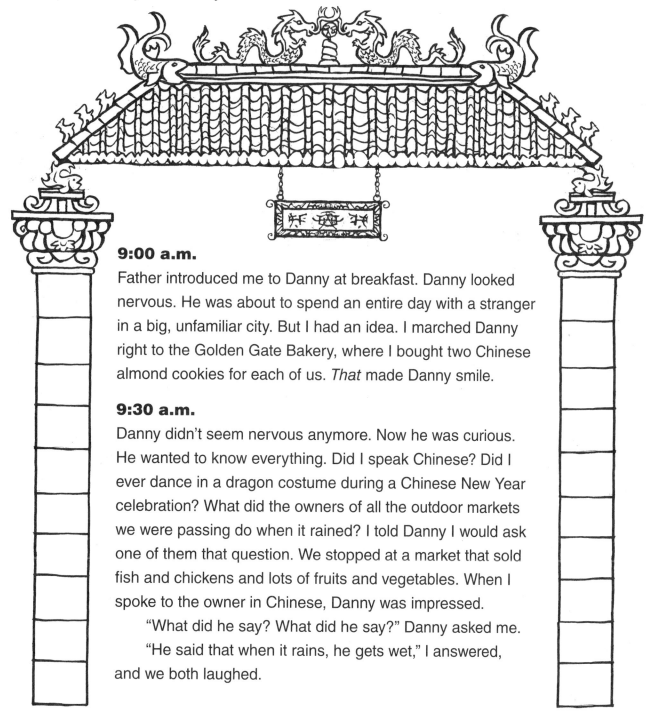

Father introduced me to Danny at breakfast. Danny looked nervous. He was about to spend an entire day with a stranger in a big, unfamiliar city. But I had an idea. I marched Danny right to the Golden Gate Bakery, where I bought two Chinese almond cookies for each of us. *That* made Danny smile.

9:30 a.m.

Danny didn't seem nervous anymore. Now he was curious. He wanted to know everything. Did I speak Chinese? Did I ever dance in a dragon costume during a Chinese New Year celebration? What did the owners of all the outdoor markets we were passing do when it rained? I told Danny I would ask one of them that question. We stopped at a market that sold fish and chickens and lots of fruits and vegetables. When I spoke to the owner in Chinese, Danny was impressed.

"What did he say? What did he say?" Danny asked me.

"He said that when it rains, he gets wet," I answered, and we both laughed.

10:00 a.m.

Now Danny was curious about Chinese art. He said that he liked the gilded storefronts and the bold black lines of the symbols on the business signs. I decided that it was time to leave Chinatown for a while. I took Danny through the famous Dragon Gates on Grant Avenue, and we made our way to the Asian Art Museum in *dai fau*—the big city. There we saw all kinds of oriental jewelry, intricate woodcarvings, and Chinese watercolor paintings.

11:00 a.m.

We went back into Chinatown, and I took Danny to the Chinese Culture Center for a history lesson. He found out that, in the 1840s, many Chinese left their homes in China because of peasant rebellions and a great famine. He was surprised that so many Chinese decided to move halfway around the world to the United States.

"The Chinese called America *Gum San,* or 'Golden Mountain,'" I told Danny as we were leaving the Chinese Culture Center. "America was thought to be full of gold and promise."

As we walked on, I explained that, at first, there were many jobs for Chinese and other immigrants. When the economy turned bad, however, the jobs dried up, and some white settlers blamed the Chinese for taking jobs away from them. Then laws were passed to keep the Chinese from moving to the United States for a while. The Chinese who already lived here stuck together through the difficult years, and Chinatown grew from a few blocks in size to a ten-block grid.

At this point, we were standing in front of beautiful old St. Mary's Church. I told Danny that early Chinese laborers who settled at Portsmouth Square had built this church by hand. We weren't far from Portsmouth Square, so I took Danny to see "the heart of Chinatown," where it first started. Looking at the historical markers and statues in the square, Danny could see that a lot of history had happened there, especially in the 1800s. Then he asked what had happened there in the 1900s.

"In 1906," I answered, "tragedy struck," and I told him about the earthquake. "Fires started all over the city, and when the fires stopped burning, Chinatown was in ruins. It took many years to rebuild and repopulate it. Today, Chinatown extends between Broadway and Bush Streets and Kearney and Stockton Streets. It's now home to more than ten thousand Chinese residents."

12:30 p.m.

Thinking about the hard work it took to build huge St. Mary's Church without modern tools must have made Danny hungry. I was ready for some lunch, too, so we went to the Bow Hon Restaurant. Danny decided to have whatever I was going to have, so I ordered two of everything—pot stickers, or boiled dumplings (which I usually eat only during Chinese New Year); wonton soup; spring rolls; and kung pao prawns. Danny was disappointed when I told him not to eat his fortune cookie, but he soon found out why.

1:30 p.m.

"Fortune cookies taste much better when they're fresh," I said, leading Danny into a fortune cookie factory.

We took the whole tour, and at the end, we ate six fortune cookies—each! Then Danny ate the cookie he had saved from Bow Hon's! One of his fortunes must have said that he would eat a lot today.

2:30 p.m.

Danny wanted to buy gifts for his family and some friends back home, so we went shopping. He found a doll for his baby sister and some red silk slippers for his mother at the Eastern Treasure Gift Shop. At another shop, he bought a wooden chess set for a friend and Chinese herbal teas for his grandmother.

4:00 p.m.

It was almost time for us to pick up some fresh fish for dinner, but we had to make one more stop. I couldn't let Danny go back to Montana without meeting my two old friends Lim and Chin. We wandered over to the Chinatown Neighborhood Center on Stockton Street. As on all Monday afternoons, Lim and Chin were playing bingo. Danny couldn't stop staring at the men's long white beards and wrinkled faces. He thought Lim and Chin must be a hundred years old! Neither one of them is older than eighty-five. They had a good laugh seeing Danny stare at their beards. Danny laughed, too.

"Bingo!" Lim yelled, and we all cheered.

4:45 p.m.

I let Danny choose the fish for dinner from an open-air market on Grant Street. We picked out fruits and vegetables, too, and Danny bought my mother some flowers. He wanted her to like him because he wants to visit us again. He told me that he wants to stay for a week next time.

"Next time," I said, "I hope you will invite me to visit Montana!"

Name ______________________

Questions About *Cheng Wan's Visitor*

1. Why might Danny have been nervous when he first arrived in Chinatown?

2. Where could Cheng and Danny have been found at 4:15 p.m.?

3. Do you think that Cheng's family eats much seafood? Explain your answer.

4. List four things that Danny learned during his day in Chinatown.

5. Do you think that Danny and Cheng enjoyed their day together? Explain your answer.

6. Why might Cheng want to visit Montana?

Name ____________________

Vocabulary Crossword

Use the words in the word box to complete the crossword puzzle.

Word Box

curious
famine
fortune
gilded
grid
herbal
immigrants
import
impressed
intricate
nervous
peasant
prawns
rebellion
residents
tragedy

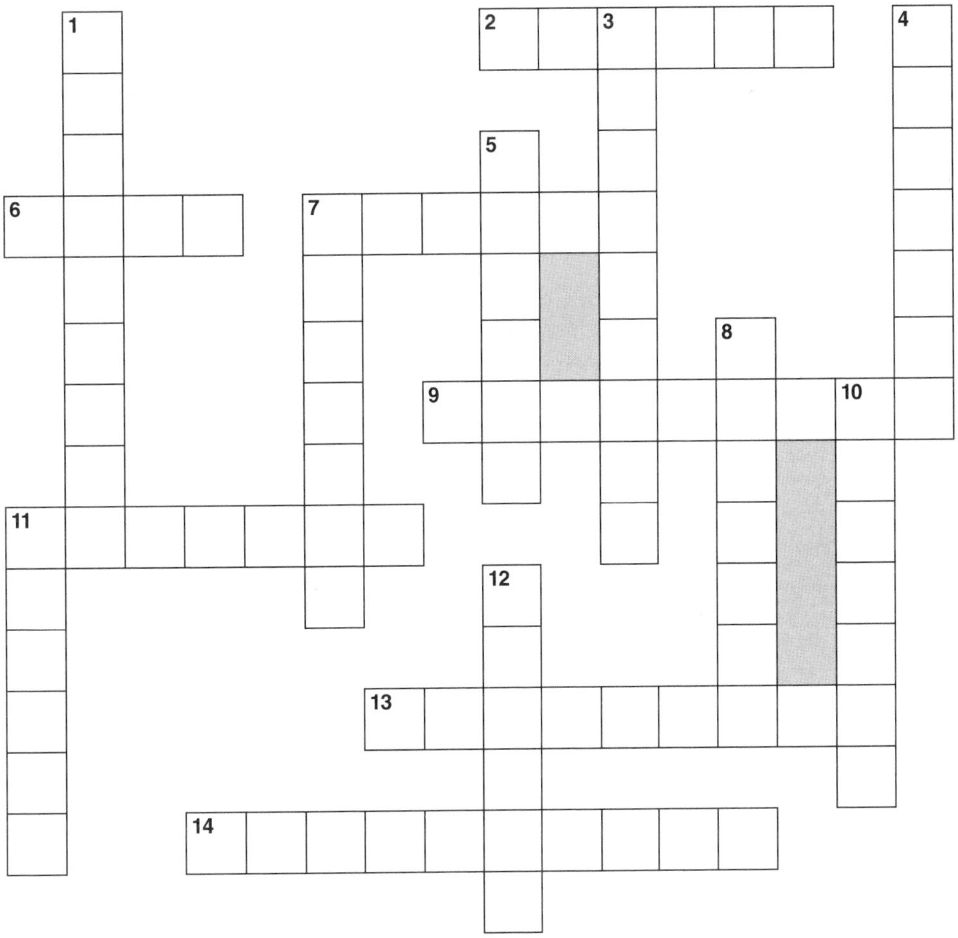

Across

2. made from plant parts that flavor foods or have medicinal value
6. a vertical and horizontal network of evenly spaced areas
7. a long and widespread shortage of food
9. the people who live at a certain place or in a certain area
11. low-paid farmworker
13. established a positive or favorable feeling
14. people who leave their own countries to live permanently in other countries

Down

1. complex and delicate
3. a violent revolt against a government or other authority
4. eager to know or find out something
5. coated or covered with gold
7. good luck or destiny
8. worried, fearful, or on edge
10. a sad event or great misfortune
11. large shrimp
12. relating to goods brought into a country from another country

Name ____________________

Write a Letter

Write a letter to both Cheng and Danny, inviting them to visit you and describing some of the places you will take them and the special things you will do together.

____

Dear Cheng and Danny,

Your friend,

____

Name ________________________________

Think About It

You are hosting a visitor from China. You have three months (and lots of money for traveling) to show your visitor what America is all about. On the lines below, list six places you would travel to and explain what you would do at each stop and why that stop is important. Use another sheet of paper if you want to include more stops.

Stop 1: ________________________________

____

____

Stop 2: ________________________________

____

____

Stop 3: ________________________________

____

____

Stop 4: ________________________________

____

____

Stop 5: ________________________________

____

____

Stop 6: ________________________________

____

____

Jesse Owens

1913–1980

Jesse Owens was born on September 12, 1913, in Alabama. His parents named him James Cleveland Owens, but his six older brothers and sisters just called him "J. C." The Owens family lived in Alabama until J. C. was nine years old. The whole family worked to earn enough money to buy food. J. C. picked cotton.

Hoping for a better life, the Owens family moved to Cleveland, Ohio. When J. C. started school there, the teacher asked him his name. He said "J. C.," but because the teacher misunderstood, she wrote down "Jesse." That name stayed with him for the rest of his life.

At East Technical High School in Cleveland, Jesse was a good student. He was also an outstanding athlete. Jesse led the track team, winning all major events three years in a row. He also set or tied national and world records in running and broad jumping.

After high school, Jesse enrolled at Ohio State University and continued his winning ways on the track. The school couldn't offer him a scholarship, so he had to work as well as study, practice, and compete. He now also had a wife to support.

When Jesse was a sophomore at Ohio State, his team went to a track meet in Michigan. Although he had injured his back, Jesse wanted to compete, and within 45 minutes' time, he tied one world record and broke some others. He tied the world record of 9.4 seconds for the 100-yard dash. He broke the world running broad jump record with a jump of 26 feet $8\frac{1}{4}$ inches. He also set a new world record in the 220-yard hurdles. His finishing time in that event was 22.6 seconds.

In 1936, Owens went to Berlin, Germany, to compete in the Olympic Games. Adolf Hitler was the head of the German government then. Hitler wanted to show the world what great athletes the Germans were. He spoke out against Jews and black people, saying that they were inferior to the Germans. Hitler was angry when Jesse Owens, the grandson of a black slave, won four gold medals that year.

Other black members of the American team also won medals for the United States, but although Hitler had congratulated many medal winners during the Games, he left the stadium to avoid congratulating Owens and the other black athletes.

Unlike Hitler, the German people cheered Owens and his outstanding performances, even when Hitler was watching. One German athlete, Luz Long, befriended Owens in spite of Hitler. After losing the gold medal to Owens in the broad jump, Luz, the silver medal winner, publicly put his arm around Jesse.

After the 1936 Olympic Games, Jesse Owens was a hero. Because he was black, however, he still faced discrimination when he returned to the United States. In spite of being one of the world's greatest athletes, he was not invited to the White House to be congratulated by the president. Like other black Americans, he had to ride in the back of city buses. He couldn't live in many neighborhoods or eat at many restaurants. Now that he was famous, however, he could earn money in professional meets and exhibitions.

People from all over the United States came to events to see the legendary Jesse Owens. Sometimes, he was even scheduled to race against animals and cars. He also toured with the Harlem Globetrotters basketball team. At times, when he didn't earn enough as an athlete, he worked as a janitor or a disk jockey.

By the time Owens was thirty-five years old, he didn't need to compete in sports events anymore. He had become a successful speaker and business consultant. He also spent a lot of time working with young people. He wanted them to have hope for making their own dreams come true.

In his later years, Jesse stopped running and jogging, but he still tried to stay physically fit by walking, lifting weights, and swimming.

Among the many awards that Owens received during his lifetime, his highest honor was the Medal of Freedom. It was presented to him in 1976 by President Gerald Ford. The Medal of Freedom is the highest honor that any American can receive.

In 1979, President Jimmy Carter honored Owens with the Living Legend Award. At long last, he was formally recognized for his achievements as both a person and an athlete. Owens died the following year on March 31.

Name ______________________________

Questions About *Jesse Owens*

1. How did James Cleveland Owens come to be called "Jesse"?

2. What were some of Owens's accomplishments as a college athlete?

3. Why didn't Adolf Hitler congratulate the black athletes who won medals at the 1936 Olympic Games?

4. Who was Luz Long? Compare his treatment of Jesse Owens to Adolf Hitler's.

5. In what ways were Owens and other black people discriminated against in the 1930s and 1940s?

6. What was the highest honor Owens received? When did he receive it?

Name ______________________

Vocabulary

A. Write each word below on the line next to its definition.

befriended	compete	discrimination	sophomore
hurdles	inferior	professional	exhibitions
legendary	recognized	consultant	formally

1. ______________ obstacles or barriers
2. ______________ special events or displays
3. ______________ singled out or given special notice for outstanding achievement
4. ______________ to participate in a contest
5. ______________ unfair or unequal treatment
6. ______________ helped someone by acting as that person's friend
7. ______________ involving payment for participating or performing
8. ______________ officially or ceremonially
9. ______________ a student in the second year of high school or college
10. ______________ lower in ability or quality
11. ______________ a person paid to provide information or advice
12. ______________ widely admired and talked about; often described as a hero

B. Write the root word for each vocabulary word below.

1. befriended ______________
2. consultant ______________
3. legendary ______________
4. professional ______________
5. exhibitions ______________
6. discrimination ______________

Name ______________________________

Think About It

A. The word "hurdles" has several meanings. Read the two meanings below and then explain how both of them apply to Jesse Owens.

1. obstacles that runners have to jump over in certain track and field events
2. problems or difficulties

____

____

____

____

____

____

____

____

B. Jesse Owens received two awards from American presidents: the Medal of Freedom and the Living Legend Award. Explain why those awards were considered higher honors than his Olympic gold medals.

____

____

____

____

____

____

____

____

Name ____________________

Write About It

Write a personal narrative about a great success you hope to achieve during your lifetime. Explain what you think you will need to do to reach your goal and describe the obstacles that you might face.

Abuelita

David knew that his grandmother, his *abuelita,* missed Mexico. As he walked with her on the beach, she talked about the mountains there and the green hills that spread out like a wrinkled blanket. She also talked about the friends she had left behind. David rattled the seashells in his pockets as he listened. With waves swirling around her feet, Abuelita stared out across the gulf toward Mexico. Their neighbor's dog had followed them on their walk, and he was whining and licking Abuelita's ankle.

"Old Dog," Abuelita said in Spanish, "are you hungry? Your master should feed you." Shaking her head, she bent down to pet him.

"I think Mrs. Bass takes good care of the dog, Abuelita," said David.

Abuelita didn't trust their neighbor, Mrs. Bass. David thought it was because Mrs. Bass didn't speak Spanish. He thought that his grandmother refused to trust anyone who didn't speak Spanish. David also thought that if his grandmother made some friends, she might be happier.

With a sad smile, Abuelita took hold of David's hand. "Let's go home and feed this poor old dog," she said in Spanish.

David and his grandmother made their way down a sandy stretch of road to the house where they lived. The dog walked along behind them and then lay down on the porch in the shade of some oleander bushes.

"I think he would like some meat," David said. "He looks like a dog that likes to eat meat."

"Sí," said Abuelita. She took some meat from the refrigerator, put it in a bowl, and set it down in front of the dog. David and his grandmother watched the old dog lick the meat hesitatingly and then whimper.

"I wonder why he isn't eating," said David.

Abuelita knelt in front of the dog and held his head in her hand. Then she began moving her fingers along the dog's jaw as if she was feeling for something. Suddenly, the dog jerked backward and growled.

"It's all right, Old Dog," she said, scratching him gently behind his ears. "I won't hurt you again."

"What's wrong with him?" David asked.

"He has a toothache, I think," said Abuelita.

Just then, the screen door slammed at Mrs. Bass's house, and David and Abuelita both heard Mrs. Bass's high-pitched voice calling for the dog.

"Gen-er-al! Gen-er-al, where are you?" she squeaked.

"He's over here, Mrs. Bass," David called back to her.

Mrs. Bass clumped up the porch steps and poked her head around the oleander bushes. "Good morning," she said with a friendly smile.

Abuelita nodded stiffly in Mrs. Bass's direction.

"Good morning, Mrs. Bass," said David. "We thought General was hungry, but he won't eat. My grandmother thinks he has a toothache."

"Really?" asked Mrs. Bass, looking at Abuelita with surprise. "I haven't been able to get poor General to eat anything either, but I didn't know what to do. He's so old that I thought... Well, I was afraid that it was something much worse. A toothache? Do you think that's all it is?"

David could tell that his grandmother was proud about figuring out the problem. Abuelita nodded to Mrs. Bass again, this time with a slight smile.

"Creo que sí," she said. "I think so," she repeated quietly in English.

Mrs. Bass looked at David with tears in her eyes. "I'm so glad it's only a toothache," she said. "I'll take General to the vet tomorrow."

Then she turned to Abuelita and said, "Thank you. I mean, *gracias*."

Without looking up, Abuelita said in English, "You are welcome."

Name ______________________

Questions About *Abuelita*

1. What is the setting of the story? Explain how you know.

2. Why did the dog jerk backward and growl when Abuelita felt along his jaw with her fingers?

3. How do you think Mrs. Bass feels about General? Support your opinion with facts from the story.

4. Why doesn't Abuelita trust Mrs. Bass?

5. What happens in the story that might lead you to believe that Abuelita will change her mind about Mrs. Bass?

6. If the story continued, what do you think would happen next?

Name ______________________

Abuelita

Synonyms

Write two synonyms for the underlined word in each sentence below.

1. Mrs. Bass clumped up the porch steps.

   ______________ ______________

2. David rattled the seashells in his pockets.

   ______________ ______________

3. Abuelita stared out across the gulf toward Mexico.

   ______________ ______________

4. The green hills spread out like a wrinkled blanket.

   ______________ ______________

5. The dog jerked backward and growled.

   ______________ ______________

6. David and his grandmother made their way down a sandy stretch of road.

   ______________ ______________

7. They watched the old dog lick the meat and then whimper.

   ______________ ______________

8. They heard Mrs. Bass's high-pitched voice.

   ______________ ______________

Say It in Spanish

Write the Spanish words from the story for the English words below.

1. grandmother ______________
2. yes ______________
3. I think so ______________
4. thank you ______________

Write About It

Abuelita felt unsure about a person who seemed different from her but then changed her mind when she started to get to know that person better. Write about a time when your feelings changed after you got to know someone. Make sure that you include how you and that person seemed different at first and what happened that made you change your mind about the person.

Name ______________________

Reading a Map

Look at the map to answer the questions below.

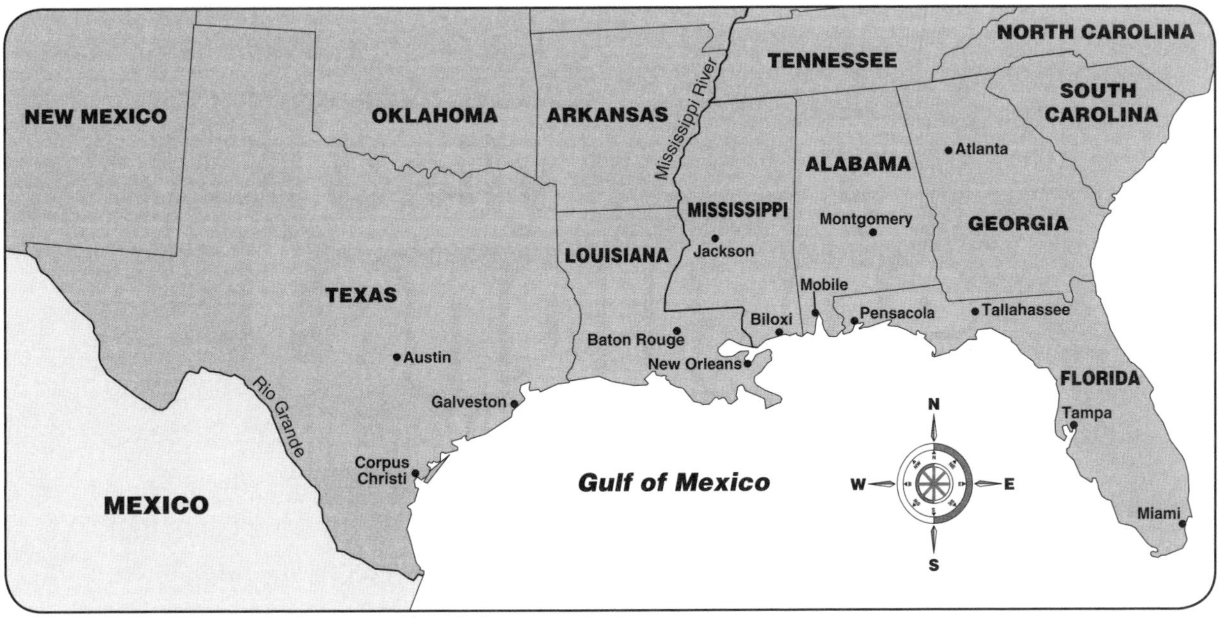

1. Which states border the Gulf of Mexico?

____

2. Which state on the Gulf of Mexico is closest to Mexico? Is it north, south, east, or west of Mexico?

____

3. Name three cities in which the story could have taken place.

____

4. A peninsula is a piece of land that is surrounded on three sides by water. Which state on the Gulf of Mexico is a peninsula?

____

5. Name two major rivers that empty into the Gulf of Mexico.

______________________ ______________________

Melting Pot

It was 11:45. Tom's history class was just ending, and everyone was eager for lunch, except Tom. He was sitting at his desk, deep in thought, only half hearing his teacher's last comment about the homework assignment.

Mrs. Grill was saying, "...and we'll make our very own melting pot right here in our classroom."

In today's history lesson, Mrs. Grill had told the class that some people call America a "melting pot" because it is made up of so many varied and wonderful cultures. She talked about the Native Americans, who were the first to inhabit the continent. She talked about the early European settlers and about African slaves who were brought to America against their will. She also talked about recent arrivals from Mexico, the Philippines, and every corner of the earth.

Then Mrs. Grill said that her class was a melting pot of its own. To show how they all meshed together to create their unique class, she had given her students an unusual homework assignment. She asked them to bring in things that represented their heritage.

"If you have nothing at home that represents your heritage, draw a picture of something that does," she said. "If you do not know where your ancestors are from, then you can bring in an item or draw a picture of something from a culture that you admire."

That last part was Tom's out, but he didn't want an out. He sullenly got up from his desk and walked to the cafeteria. His best friend, Carlos, saw him coming and waited at the cafeteria door.

"Hi, Carlos," Tom said, without his usual enthusiasm.

"Hi," Carlos responded in a puzzled tone. "What's wrong, Tom?"

"Mrs. Grill's assignment," Tom replied. "We're supposed to bring something for our class melting pot tomorrow, but I don't want to bring something from a culture that I just admire. I want to bring something from my own heritage. I want to know my own ancestors. I at least want to know my own parents."

Carlos knew that Tom had been adopted. Carlos had been adopted, too, but Carlos knew who his parents were. His mother even visited once in a while, and his dad always sent birthday gifts. Carlos had been adopted by his grandparents when he was two years old. His parents were unable to take care of him, but they were not entirely out of the picture.

Tom had never known his biological parents. He loved his adoptive parents and wouldn't trade a day of his life for the life of any other person. Still, he couldn't help wondering about his real background.

"Tom," said Carlos, "I don't know anything about your ancestors, and it doesn't bother me one bit. All I know is that you're my best friend, and you always will be. Here, have one of my grandma's famous sugar cookies. Maybe that will cheer you up."

Tom took the cookie, but he didn't feel like eating it.

At the dinner table that evening, Tom asked his mom and dad about their backgrounds. They were both German. Tom's mother told him that he could take her favorite nutcracker to school for the melting pot.

Later, Tom walked to his neighbor Jenny's house. Jenny said her family was from Jamaica, and she gave Tom her favorite seashell from her family's trip there last summer.

"Maybe this could go into your melting pot," she said.

On his way back home, Tom ran into another neighbor, but four-year-old Kevin didn't know anything about his ancestors.

"What does 'Aunt Sisters' mean, anyway?" he asked Tom.

"Never mind, Kevin," Tom replied, walking away.

"Tom!" Kevin yelled after him. "You can have one of my frogs!"

Tom took the frog from Kevin and grinned.

"Thanks, buddy," he said and walked on home.

That night, Tom had a wonderful dream, and the next morning, he got onto the school bus with a big smile and a medium-sized box.

Tom kept the box on the floor next to his desk until history class began and Mrs. Grill asked for contributions to the melting pot. The melting pot was a big kettle that Mrs. Grill had borrowed from the cafeteria. Tom watched as his classmates put in drawings, knickknacks, keepsakes, and even junk.

Marcella added a wedge of cheese that had been imported from France. Her father was French. Ling put in a beautiful kite made of silk and bamboo, with a colorful dragon embroidered on it. His uncle, who still lives in China, brought it as a gift for Ling on a visit to America a few years ago.

Tom and his box were the last to reach the melting pot.

"Mrs. Grill," he said, "I want to add myself to the melting pot of Room 403. I am proud to be a melting pot made up of all the nice people I meet every day. I may not know my own heritage, but my friends have shared their heritages with me."

Tom opened his box and put his mother's nutcracker into the big kettle. Then he added Jenny's seashell. Next came Carlos's grandma's sugar cookie. Finally, Tom reached into his box and added one plump green frog to the kettle.

The class laughed and cheered. As everyone gathered around the melting pot to see the frog, Tom only half heard his teacher say, "Before anyone goes to lunch, I think we should take that last addition to the creek behind the school and set it free."

Name ________________________

Questions About *Melting Pot*

1. Why was Tom unhappy after his history class ended?

2. Why might Tom have wanted to know about his heritage?

3. Tom's best friend, Carlos, also had been adopted. How did Carlos know about his heritage?

4. What could students who didn't know anything about their ancestors add to Mrs. Grill's melting pot?

5. Why is the United States sometimes called a "melting pot"?

6. What do you think Tom meant when he said that he was a melting pot all by himself?

Name ______________________

Vocabulary

A. Use clues from the story to define the phrases below in your own words.

1. *melting pot* (paragraph 2) ______________________

2. *recent arrivals* (paragraph 3) ______________________

3. *Tom's out* (paragraph 6) ______________________

4. *out of the picture* (paragraph 10) ______________________

5. *biological parents* (paragraph 11) ______________________

6. *adoptive parents* (paragraph 11) ______________________

7. *that last addition* (last sentence of the story) ______________________

B. Write each word below on the line next to the correct synonym. Use a dictionary if you need help understanding the meanings of the words.

sullen	knickknacks	culture	mesh
keepsake	enthusiasm	comment	heritage

1. eagerness ______________________
2. civilization ______________________
3. souvenir ______________________
4. interlock ______________________
5. glum ______________________
6. ancestry ______________________
7. ornaments ______________________
8. remark ______________________

Name ____________________

Write About It

The story says that Tom had a wonderful dream, and when he woke up the next morning, he knew what he was going to add to his class's melting pot. On the lines below, write what you think Tom might have dreamed.

Your Own Melting Pot

1. Describe your family's background or heritage if you know it. Include where your ancestors came from and explain how their lifestyles and traditions have shaped your life. (If you do not know about your own heritage, write about how the backgrounds or lifestyles of the people close to you have shaped your life.)

2. Describe five items you would put into your own melting pot and explain how each item reflects the people and events that have shaped your life.

The Story Game

My great-grandma Bonnie is ninety-two years old. I am ten and three-quarters. When I visit my Grandma Bonnie, we play a story game. We play it all afternoon. Grandma Bonnie always starts the game. She says…

"When I was ten and three-quarters years old… the summer air was so terrifically hot that the humidity made me feel like I was swimming in my own backyard, even after the sun went down. On Saturday nights, my mother would give me ten cents so I could walk to town and buy an ice-cream cone and a bag of popcorn. I'd eat them while I listened to a band play from an old bandwagon that parked outside the bank."

Then I say… *"Once, I listened to a band play. It was on an enormous stage that was equipped with wireless microphones, two-story-high speakers, neon lights, and billowy smoke. They didn't serve ice-cream cones or popcorn there, but that's okay, because they would have cost a lot more than ten cents."*

And then Grandma Bonnie goes again.

"When I was ten and three-quarters years old… I was in the fifth grade. Every weekday morning, I jumped onto a wagon that stopped outside our house. Then the driver drove the horses through the middle of town to pick up the West End kids. We all had to go to school in the basement of the Garrett Library because our town was getting bigger every year and there wasn't room for all of us in the old four-room schoolhouse anymore."

"Hey, Grandma, I'm in the fifth grade, too! I ride in a yellow bus to a brand-new school. The school is so big that I don't think there could ever be too many kids to fit in it. I sure hope not, anyway, because our town library doesn't have a basement."

"When I was ten and three-quarters years old… I lived with my mom and my dad and my two brothers and two sisters at 1301 West Quincy Street. We had a large house that my father built all by himself. It had a kitchen, a living room, a dining room, two bedrooms downstairs, and three more bedrooms upstairs. Outdoors is where we went to the privy."

"Well, I live at 153 Cottage Court with my mom and my little brother. We have a lot of rooms, too, but we can go to the bathroom indoors."

"When I was ten and three-quarters years old… I helped my father in our garden, hoeing potatoes and weeding onions. Then I helped him chop wood to use in our cookstove. I'd also gather eggs from the chickens and help the iceman carry a big block of ice to our icebox. On some days, I'd help my mother sew underclothes or cook a meal or do the laundry. I had to scrub the clothes by hand on a washboard."

"Mom and I planted a small garden this summer. Sometimes, I bake cookies or throw laundry into the washing machine, but I definitely do not sew my own underwear, and our refrigerator works quite nicely without a block of ice."

"When I was ten and three-quarters years old… I got sick with a sore throat, and my mother made me gargle a mixture of salt, pepper, and vinegar. Then she wrapped a strip of bacon around my neck. While I was lying in bed resting, my cat jumped on me and started chewing on the bacon!"

"When I have a sore throat, my mom gives me herbal tea and pink medicine. Then I just lie on the couch all day and watch TV or play video games."

"When I was ten and three-quarters years old… my favorite time of day was after my father got home from work. We all ate dinner together, and then Father played with us for a while. One night, he was chasing us kids on his hands and knees, and my little brother picked up a wooden spoon and hit him over the head. A big knot formed on Father's head, and then that was the end of that game!"

"When we go to Dad's house, we play basketball in the driveway, but my little brother hasn't hit Dad on the head with the ball yet. Dad always catches it."

Whenever Great-Grandma Bonnie starts to tell me about something that Great-Great-Grandpa Miller taught her how to do, I know that our story game is almost over.

"When I was ten and three-quarters years old… my father taught me how to make a kite. We used sticks from the yard, old newspapers, and paste that I could make myself out of flour and water."

"Will you show me how to make a kite, Grandma?" I ask.

Sometimes, it isn't a kite. Sometimes, it's homemade ice cream or a wooden car or a clothespin doll, but Grandma's answer is always the same…

"Yes, I will!"

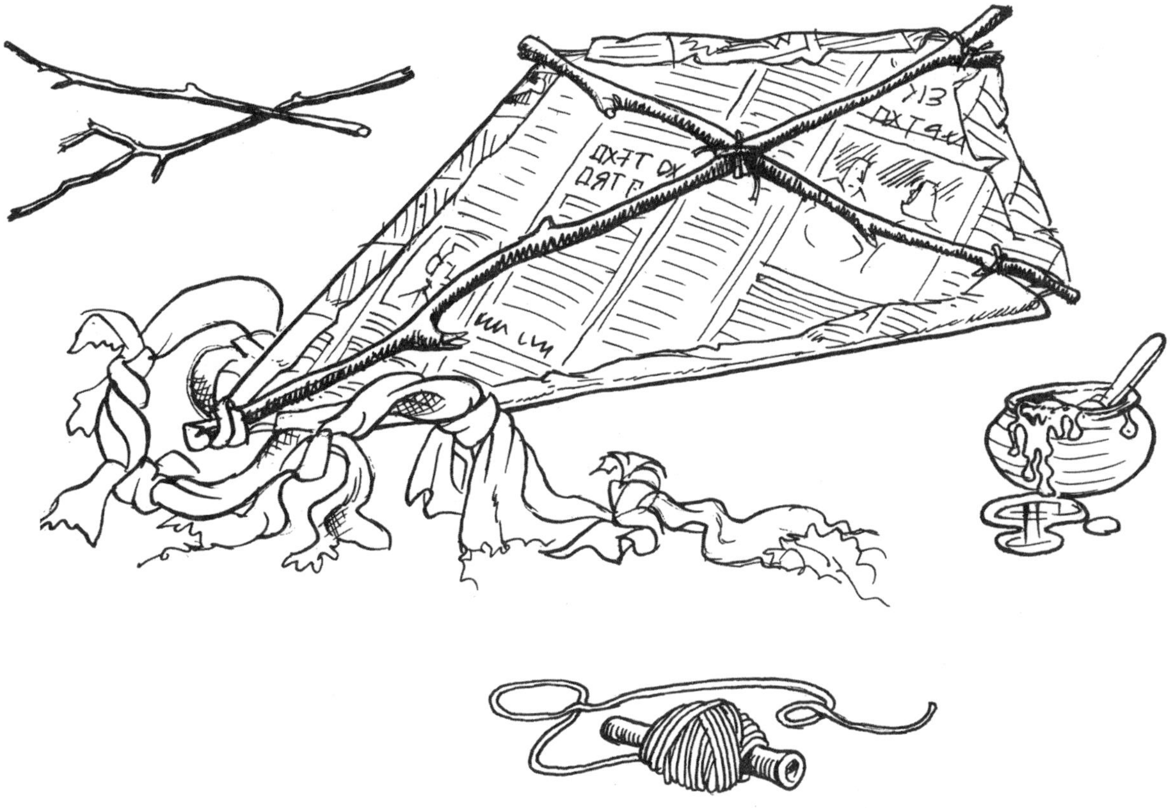

Name ______________________

Questions About *The Story Game*

1. In the story, a young girl and her great-grandmother play a special game whenever they're together. Explain the game they play.

____

____

____

2. Great-Grandma Bonnie has lived ninety-two years. What are some of the changes the story hints at that Grandma Bonnie has seen the world go through during her lifetime?

____

____

____

____

3. What were some of Grandma Bonnie's chores as a young girl? How do they compare to her great-granddaughter's chores?

____

____

____

4. At the end of the story game, the girl and her great-grandmother make a kite. Do you think the girl knew that they would complete a project together? Explain your answer.

____

____

____

Name ____________________

Vocabulary

Use a dictionary to find definitions for the following words. After each word, write the abbreviation for the correct part of speech. Then write the meaning of the word as it is used in the story.

Example: humidity __n.__ __water vapor in the air__

n. = noun **v. = verb** **adj. = adjective** **adv. = adverb**

1. terrifically ______ ____________________

____

2. equipped ______ ____________________

____

3. neon ______ ____________________

____

4. washboard ______ ____________________

____

5. billowy ______ ____________________

____

6. definitely ______ ____________________

____

7. gargle ______ ____________________

____

8. privy ______ ____________________

____

9. herbal ______ ____________________

____

Name ______________________

Ask Great-Grandma Bonnie

A. Write five questions that you would ask Great-Grandma Bonnie about her childhood in the early 1900s.

1. ____

____

2. ____

____

3. ____

____

4. ____

____

5. ____

____

B. Would you like to have Great-Grandma Bonnie as your own great-grandmother? Explain why or why not.

____

____

____

____

____

____

____

____

Name ______________________

Now and Then

Ask a friend or a relative who is at least fifty years old about the main forms of communication, transportation, and recreation when he or she was your age. Then answer the same questions yourself and write the information in the boxes below to compare **now** and **then**.

Now	Then
Your Name: ______________________ **Age:** ________	**Person's Name:** ______________________ **Age:** ________
Communication:	**Communication:**
Transportation:	**Transportation:**
Recreation:	**Recreation:**

Comparing Texts

Along with building background and activating prior knowledge or experience, comparing texts is an important reading strategy that aids and improves reading comprehension. The focus of this reading strategy is making connections. In comparing texts, students make text-to-text connections based on what they read.

Comparing texts is a heavily tested reading objective that promotes both literary analysis and critical thinking skills. By making text-to-text connections, students

- learn how to compare and contrast literary elements such as characters, plot, theme, and setting;
- better understand individual texts by seeing them juxtaposed with one another; and
- practice higher-order critical and creative thinking.

The activities on the following pages ask students to think about two stories and then answer questions that compare the texts. The activities are suitable for both group instruction and independent practice (see page 4). Before comparing the texts, students must have read both of the stories and should have completed some or all of their related skill pages.

Name ______________________

Where in the World? and *Cheng Wan's Visitor*

1. How are the two stories alike? Fill in the circle next to the correct answer.
   Ⓐ Both stories include a tour of a place.
   Ⓑ Both stories are mostly about the history of a place.
   Ⓒ Both stories are mostly about the physical features of a place.

2. Describe how the following elements in one story are different from the other story.

   Setting: ______________________

   Characters: ______________________

   Action: ______________________

3. Fill in the correct circle to answer each question.

   Ⓐ = *Where in the World?*   Ⓑ = *Cheng Wan's Visitor*

   a. Which story takes place in one day? Ⓐ Ⓑ
   b. Which story includes the reader as a character? Ⓐ Ⓑ
   c. Which story is narrated by one of the characters? Ⓐ Ⓑ
   d. Which story has a South American setting? Ⓐ Ⓑ
   e. Which story includes an island location? Ⓐ Ⓑ
   f. Which story includes facts about history and culture? Ⓐ Ⓑ

4. After reading each story, which place would you rather visit? Explain why.

   ____

Name ______________________________

Maria Tallchief and Jesse Owens

1. How are the two stories alike? Fill in the circle next to the correct answer.
   Ⓐ They are both fiction.
   Ⓑ They are both journals.
   Ⓒ They are both biographies.

2. What can you learn from the life of...

   Maria Tallchief? ______________________________

   ____

   Jesse Owens? ______________________________

   ____

3. How are Maria Tallchief's and Jessie Owens's achievements similar?

   ____

   ____

4. Maria Tallchief and Jesse Owens both had to overcome obstacles to achieve their goals. Who had a more difficult time becoming successful? Use facts from the stories to support your answer.

   ____

   ____

5. Choose a different adjective to describe each person. Explain your choice.

   determined legendary proud strong

   Maria Tallchief: ______________________________

   ____

   Jesse Owens: ______________________________

   ____

Name ____________________________

The Warrior and the Princess and The One-Inch Boy

1. A legend is a type of folk tale that explains something in nature. Which of these two folk tales is a legend and what does it explain?

____

____

2. Some common elements found in folk tales are listed below. Write the letter for each element in the correct section of the Venn diagram.

a. a journey	e. a beautiful daughter	i. a disguise
b. an ogre	f. a handsome young man	j. a marriage
c. a charm	g. a misunderstanding	k. a wish comes true
d. a test	h. a change into something else	l. living happily ever after

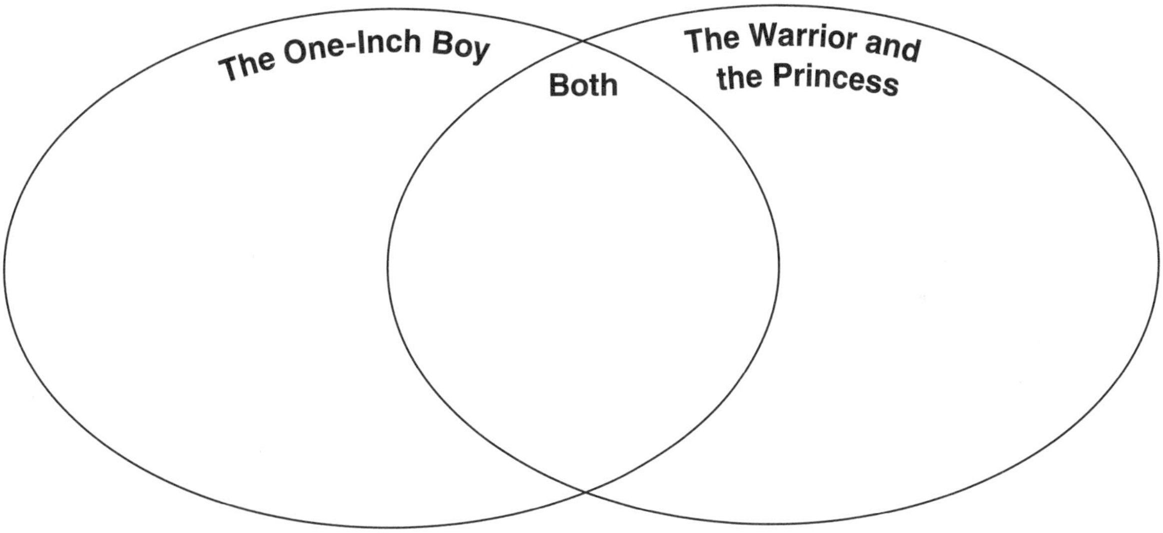

3. In a folk tale, the main character has to prove himself or herself. Explain how the main character in each of these folk tales proves himself.

Prince Popo: ____

____

____

One-Inch Boy: ____

____

____

Name ______________________

Vietnamese Holidays and Dancing to the Drum

1. How are the two stories alike? Fill in the circle next to the correct answer.
   - Ⓐ They are both folk tales.
   - Ⓑ They are both articles.
   - Ⓒ They are both realistic fiction.

2. Use the following categories to describe how a Tet celebration differs from a powwow.

   food: ______________________

   ____

   music: ______________________

   ____

   decorations: ______________________

   ____

   why celebrated: ______________________

   ____

3. Which of the following characteristics of celebrations are important for **both** Tet and powwows? Check all that apply.

   - ☐ religious activities
   - ☐ honoring ancestors
   - ☐ games and contests
   - ☐ music and dancing
   - ☐ special foods
   - ☐ entertaining guests
   - ☐ costumes
   - ☐ gift-giving
   - ☐ large public gatherings

4. Which celebration seems more fun—Tet or a powwow? Include details from the stories to support your opinion.

   ____

   ____

   ____

   ____

Name ___________________________

Amazing Ants! and *Beaks and Feathers*

1. Compare the information in the stories. Write **ants**, **birds**, or **both** on the line.

   Which story...

   a. shows what the animals look like? ______________

   b. focuses on the animals' physical features? ______________

   c. tells how the animals get their food? ______________

   d. provides many details about the animals' homes? ______________

   e. uses a diagram to give information? ______________

   f. explains how the animals work together? ______________

   g. explains the molting process? ______________

   h. compares different species of the animal? ______________

2. Name one thing that is similar and one thing that is different about the homes of South American rainforest ants and the homes of flamingos.

   ____

   ____

   ____

3. Name one thing you learned from each story that helps you understand how the animals survive in their habitats.

   ____

   ____

   ____

   ____

   ____

   ____

Answer Key

Page 9

1. He slept in a hammock that his mother knitted for him. It stretched from a giant pine tree in New Bedford, Massachusetts, to an enormous chestnut tree in Newport, Rhode Island.
2. He was too big to fit on any other ship. His ship was the biggest ship that ever sailed the ocean.
3. He named his ship the *Colossus,* because the word means "gigantic" or "enormous."
4. The ship ran into the tip of South America, breaking it into many islands and creating a strait.
5. Throughout his life, Stormalong was always kind, considerate, and helpful to people, animals, and the earth.
6. Answers will vary but should include information about the hurricane, rescuing ships and seamen, and Stormalong's trip into the sky.

Page 10

A.
1. starboard
2. hammock
3. steeple
4. halibut
5. port
6. strait
7. latter
8. christened
9. former
10. anchored

B.
1. unfurled
2. raged
3. tremendous
4. immense
5. exquisite

Page 11

A.
1. hurry, greet
2. named
3. build
4. hired
5. ripped

B.
1. shouted
2. goodbye
3. starboard
4. latter
5. sea
6. crowded

Page 12

Stormalong was a big baby.
He outgrew his cradle in a week. When he was a year old, he had to sleep in the barn because the house was too small. At two years old, he was taller than the church steeple.

Stormalong built his own ship.
He chopped down trees from every forest between the Atlantic coast and Pennsylvania. He sloshed through the ocean carrying fish from ships to all the towns along the shore, and the water never came up past his knees.

Stormalong didn't need a crew.
He taught himself everything there was to know about map reading, math, and the stars. He could do everything a hundred seamen could do and faster.

Stormalong rescued ships and sailors from a hurricane.
He swam through towering waves. He pulled sailors from the water and put them safely on his ship. He piled up their ships on the deck of the *Colossus*. He swam to Florida, pulling his ship along by holding the anchor chain between his teeth.

Page 15

1. The date when Tet begins depends on the cycles of the moon.
2. The family sets up an altar and puts pictures of the ancestors on it, along with food, candles, and incense. The family invites the souls of the ancestors to share New Year's Eve dinner with them.
3. People want to please the kitchen god so he will take good reports about their families to the Jade Emperor in heaven.
4. a. January, February
   b. three, seven
   c. kind, arguments
   d. cleaned, decorated, blossoms
5. The Vietnamese believe that the first visitor of the new year brings good luck or bad luck. By choosing the visitor, a family can make sure that it is someone who will bring good luck to the household.

Page 16

A.
1. pagoda
2. incense
3. ancestor
4. lunar
5. spirits
6. lotus
7. altar
8. national
9. ceremony
10. cycle
11. preserved
12. Tet

B. List can include any six of the following foods:
moon cakes, preserved fruits, lotus seeds, noodles, rice cakes, beans, pork dumplings

Page 17

m	r	h	v	c	r	m	p	a	r	a	d	e	o
p	j	o	i	p	t	b	t	g	t	p	m	z	n
c	e	l	e	b	r	a	t	e	u	a	o	b	t
x	a	i	t	a	n	a	j	q	s	l	o	a	r
p	l	d	n	t	i	n	y	e	f	e	n	l	h
k	t	a	r	n	c	v	s	e	o	t	s	i	g
z	l	y	m	g	e	r	s	p	r	i	n	g	t
t	e	m	p	l	e	s	z	k	t	s	l	m	e
s	o	l	g	m	p	w	e	r	u	m	o	k	s
t	c	w	e	x	l	r	h	o	n	o	r	s	t
f	i	r	e	c	r	a	c	k	e	r	s	n	h

Sentences will vary.

Page 18

Answers will vary.

I. A. Children parade with lanterns.
B. People admire the moon.
C. People eat moon cakes.

II. A. Buddhists honor their founder.
B. Captive birds and fish are set free.

III. A. People go to temples and pagodas to pray.

B. Children are given red envelopes with gifts of money inside.

C. Everyone enjoys treats made of preserved fruits and lotus seeds.

D. Families invite special visitors to bring good fortune to their households.

E. Small villages often celebrate with traditional songs and dances and special activities.

IV. A. People place pictures to honor their ancestors.

B. Pictures are surrounded with candles and incense.

C. Food is set out.

D. Families invite the spirits of their ancestors to share the New Year's Eve dinner.

V. A. is honored with a special offering to make him happy

B. gives reports about families to the Jade Emperor in heaven

C. If pleased, he praises the family.

Page 21

1. the individual medley at a swim meet
2. Answers will vary, but should include some of the following words or their synonyms: anxious, prepared, conditioned, ready, confident
3. a. butterfly c. breast stroke
   b. backstroke d. freestyle
4. He saw the flags overhead that signaled the end of the pool.
5. "He was the winner" could also mean that he did his best, gave it his all, or had prepared himself as thoroughly as he could.
6. Answers will vary.

Page 22

A. 5, 6, 1, 4, 3, 2

B. 1. B
2. A
3. C
4. A

Page 23

A. Answers may be any eight of the following verbs and verb phrases: flew down the lane, broke the surface, slicing into the water, reached, pulled, glided, jerked in a frog kick, pressed forward, powered off, slid through the water

B. Verbs and sentences will vary. Examples of verbs include: amble, march, saunter, shuffle, step, stroll, waddle

Page 24

1. **simile:** His arms turned like the blades of a windmill… (compares Mark's arms to a windmill's blades)
2. **metaphor:** He was potential energy personified. (compares Mark to contained energy); a speeding missile bound for the finish. (compares Mark to a speeding missile)

personification: The rough texture bit into his fingertips. (gives a wall the ability to bite)

Page 28

1. She liked talking to her and listening to her stories about the past and about Sally's mom. She also liked that G-G-Ma always had time to listen to her, laugh at her jokes, and give her hugs, whether she needed them or not.
2. They had baked a cake, Sally's mom was going to make G-G-Ma's favorite dinner, and Sally had made a card and written a poem to go with it.
3. G-G-Ma already had everything she needed—sweaters, aprons, towels, clothes, knickknacks, figurines.
4. Answers should include the idea that if the kitten stayed outside, it would be more likely to find a home or to be found by someone who could take care of it.
5. Sally already had a big, lively dog, and her mom had told her that she could have only one pet.
6. Sally convinced her mother that G-G-Ma should have the kitten and that they could help her take care of it. Sally's mother bought the supplies that G-G-Ma needed for the kitten and made plans to take the kitten to the vet for a checkup.

Page 29

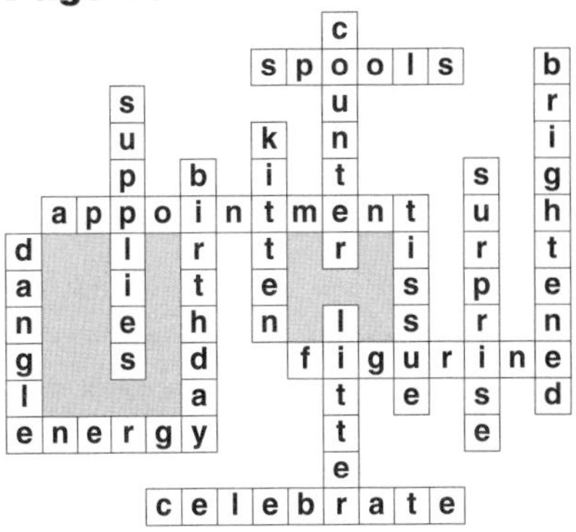

Page 30

1. doorknob
2. everywhere
3. leftover
4. empty-handed
5. knickknacks
6. great-grandma
7. outside
8. sometimes
9. ninety-one
10. checkup

1. to
2. too
3. too
4. to

Page 31

Experiences and comparisons will vary.

Page 34

1. Answers may be any three of the following:
   clean and feed the queen
   care for the queen's eggs and the larvae
   go out to collect food
   take care of or enlarge the colony's living quarters
2. Ants farm fungi. They chew leaves to make a paste and then spread the paste inside the colony's rooms to fertilize the fungi and help them grow.
3. They are a source of food.
4. Honeydew is a sticky sap that ants use for food. Aphids give off the sap when herder ants stroke the sides of the insects.
5. The guards keep out ants that don't belong to the community and that will try to kidnap larvae and raise them to be slaves in their own communities.
6. in bamboo or other hollow plants

Page 35

i, g, k, b, h, l, d, f, j, a, c, n, e, m

c, e, b, a, d

Page 36

1. aphids
2. bamboo
3. carpenter
4. chewer
5. colony
6. exoskeleton
7. fungi
8. harvester
9. herder
10. honeydew
11. larvae
12. leafcutter
13. mound
14. saliva
15. subterranean
16. tunnel

m	o	u	n	d	z	s	p	h	r	z	s
s	q	k	r	m	d	h	v	e	f	y	u
b	s	a	l	i	v	a	d	q	l	h	b
i	l	z	h	e	d	r	m	b	a	o	t
v	d	p	t	o	e	v	r	j	r	n	e
c	a	o	l	h	m	e	s	e	v	e	r
s	b	r	u	t	w	s	t	p	a	y	r
c	a	r	p	e	n	t	e	r	e	d	a
o	m	y	h	x	u	e	m	t	g	e	n
l	b	c	j	c	k	r	f	u	n	w	e
o	o	z	f	u	n	g	i	n	v	s	a
n	o	a	t	r	f	o	s	n	d	k	n
y	e	x	o	s	k	e	l	e	t	o	n
l	v	c	s	y	i	u	m	l	w	g	k

Page 37

1. type
2. subterranean
3. dig
4. enlarge
5. gather
6. enormous
7. build
8. kidnap
9. stroking
10. guards

1. fungi
2. larvae
3. leaves
4. communities

Page 41

1. No suitors pleased both Ixtli and her father, the emperor.
2. He wanted to be near Ixtli to find out what kind of person she was.
3. He found out that she was as kind as she was beautiful.
4. He came from a poor kingdom, and it took time for him to gather treasures worthy of the princess to give to her father when asking for permission to marry her.
5. The emperor called Popo the "prince of nothing" and said that Popo was not worthy to rule the emperor's kingdom.
6. She died of grief when she thought Popo had been killed and would never return.

Page 42

Page 43

Consider all reasonable answers, but they should at least include the following:

Emperor: angry, rich, powerful

Princess Ixtli: beautiful, kind, gentle, caring, loving, worried, grieving

Prince Popo: brave, strong, loving, loyal, worthy

1. Her eyes were a soft brown like the eyes of the deer…
2. a. Answers will vary.
   b. Answers will vary.
3. Answers will vary.
   Examples:
   as strong as **an ox**
   as sly as **a fox**
   as stubborn as **a mule**
   as quiet as **a mouse**
   works like **a horse**
   stings like **a bee**
   swims like **a fish**
   runs like **a deer**

Page 44

Answers will vary, but they should include reasons similar to the following:

1. The story starts with "In ancient times," and the setting, characters, and references to kingdoms and invaders are common to stories from times long past.
2. The story takes place in a real country (Mexico) and features real landforms (the volcanic mountains Popocatepetl and Ixtaccihuatl)
3. All of the story's characters are human, although the princess's beauty and goodness is somewhat exaggerated. So is the situation when she dies of grief on the very day Popo returns. Popo's gardener disguise to "spy" on the princess, the lengths he goes to so he will be worthy of the princess, and his great success as a warrior also seem exaggerated.
4. Popo must first make sure that the princess is as good as she is beautiful. Then he must prove to the emperor that he is worthy to marry the princess. He must also accumulate treasures and win battles against invading enemies.
5. Ixtli's death and Popo's actions following it are meant to explain the existence of two mountains in Mexico: Popocatepetl and Ixtaccihuatl.

Page 47

1. warmblooded
   vertebrates
   two wings
   two scaly legs
   a beak
   feathers
2. Molting is the process of shedding and growing back large amounts of hair or feathers at regular intervals. Birds molt to replace old, damaged feathers with new, healthy ones.
3. An owl can turn its head around far enough to see directly behind itself. Because the owl's eyes don't move in the eye sockets, this feature helps the owl see things that are not directly in front of it.
4. The pink coloring in the shrimp and algae flamingos eat passes through their bodies and colors their feathers different shades of pink.
5. It has to empty the water out of its pouch and then swallow the fish it caught.
6. Some parrots use their beaks as a third foot to help them climb trees.

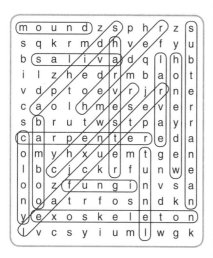

Page 48

A. 1. plumage
2. talons
3. species
4. exotic
5. vertebrates
6. molt
7. raptors
8. sieve

B. Answers will vary. Possible answers include:

owl–has talons, excellent vision, and fringed feathers on its wings for silent flight

flamingo–has a beak like a sieve for straining the water out of its food

pelican–has an expanding pouch on its beak to hold fish

parrot–has a strong beak and a thick tongue for eating fruits, nuts, and seeds; may use its beak as a third foot for climbing

Page 49

1. a. school**'s**
   b. Penguin**s'**
   c. woman**'s**
   d. horse**s'**
   e. player**s'**
   f. brother**'s**
2. bird's, species', Birds', seedeater's, woodpecker's, owl's, flamingo's, parrot's
3. Birds'
4. Sentences will vary, but possessives must be formed and used correctly.

Page 50

1. Answers will vary. Possible answer: All birds have certain characteristics in common.
2. Answers will vary. Possible answer: The different physical characteristics of birds help them adjust to their environments.
3. Answers will vary. Possible answer: In order to survive, birds have learned to eat the food that is available in their habitats.

Answers will vary.

Page 54

1. It was taken over by pet worms that were eating everything.
2. All the other planets were too crowded.
3. dispose of them in a black hole
4. Answers may be any four of the following activities: read, watch TV, look out at the scenery, work in the garden, work in the science lab, go air swimming, take space walks
5. The narrator mentions having run out of books to read and not having seen a library for five years. Also, the first thing the narrator asked after landing on the new planet was for directions to a library.
6. Answers will vary. Possible answer: in a city park on the planet Earth
7. They saw the skeletons of creatures similar to themselves, and they were being chased by creatures with nets.

Page 55

1. Noxious
2. plagued
3. mingle
4. etiquette
5. deserted
6. hitched
7. disposing
8. garbled
9. blasted
10. transmitted
11. resumed
12. system

Page 56

noxious: 2
asteroid: 3
miniaturized: 5
scenery: 3
plagued: 1
meteor: 3
communication: 5
transporter: 3
intergalactic: 5
satellite: 3
populated: 4
museum: 3
antigravity: 5
skeletons: 3
monitor: 3

a	l	d	t	r	a	n	s	p	o	r	t	e	r	k	r
c	o	m	m	u	n	i	c	a	t	i	o	n	l	o	t
e	s	x	i	t	a	y	e	d	p	l	n	g	t	i	x
r	k	a	q	c	n	i	n	j	n	o	x	i	o	u	s
s	e	t	i	l	t	o	e	b	z	s	n	n	g	a	d
m	l	t	e	c	i	s	r	m	n	o	l	t	p	i	a
a	e	s	y	k	g	l	y	e	m	e	t	e	o	r	d
u	t	l	m	u	r	o	l	s	g	n	o	r	a	e	u
p	o	p	u	l	a	t	e	d	o	l	e	g	y	s	d
l	n	u	s	a	v	h	t	z	i	t	u	a	r	g	e
a	s	n	e	y	i	c	h	o	s	r	p	l	i	z	m
g	r	a	u	v	t	i	l	a	c	t	i	a	x	u	s
u	t	l	m	g	y	s	a	t	e	x	o	c	n	d	p
e	r	o	i	c	s	a	t	e	l	l	i	t	e	s	a
d	c	a	n	m	i	n	i	a	t	u	r	i	z	e	d
o	r	z	p	e	n	k	s	p	v	r	t	c	d	l	a

Page 57

1. Mom said that the Maiasaura looked like her Aunt Worima. And when they saw the picture of the Psittacosaurus, the narrator said, "There must be others here just like us," and Dad agreed and said, "That's us."
2. Answers will vary, but three different possibilities must be listed. Possible answers:
   1) They were captured and put on display in the museum.
   2) They made friends with the creatures on the new planet.
   3) They fought with the creatures, overpowered them, and took control of the new planet.
3. Endings will vary but must include the Worims being captured.

Page 61

1. He could crawl under chairs and tables to find lost objects.

   He brought in grass that could be woven into mats or shoes.

   He helped his father look for fallen branches that could be used for firewood.
2. Answers will vary but must be an activity that requires being tall and strong.
3. He wanted to seek his fortune.
4. His boat was a small bowl; the oars were pieces of chopsticks. He had a sewing needle for a sword and a piece of straw for a scabbard.
5. Being so small, he was able to get inside the ogre's body and hurt him from inside.
6. The noble rewarded One-Inch Boy with half of all his lands and wealth.
7. He brought his parents to Kyoto to live in the palace with him.

Page 62

A.
1. charmed
2. scabbard
3. dense
4. swamped
5. ogre
6. transformed
7. journey
8. persisted
9. lacquer
10. bore

B.
1. unsheathed
2. marveled
3. fortune
4. coincidence
5. tremendous

Page 63

Part 1: 3, 1, 4, 2, 5

Part 2: 5, 1, 3, 4, 2

Part 3: 2, 5, 3, 1, 4

Page 64

1. Answers will vary. Possible answer: His parents loved him and wanted to help him achieve his dream.
2. Answers will vary. Possible answer: The boatman was a kind and caring person.
3. Answers will vary. Possible answer: The people in the palace liked One-Inch Boy and enjoyed being with him.
4. Answers will vary. Possible answer: One-Inch Boy was very brave, and, despite his size, was clever enough to defend himself and help others.
5. Answers will vary. Possible answer: The noble was a generous person and was grateful to One-Inch Boy.

Page 67

1. pen or pencil, ruler, scissors, glue, empty cardboard tube from paper towels, plain paper or wrapping paper, decorative items such as ribbon, glitter, stickers, and sequins
2. Glue isn't needed. Self-adhesive paper has its own glue (adhesive) on one side.
3. Answers may vary but should include that they help decorate the table for special events.
4. Put a loose or folded paper or cloth napkin through each ring and then arrange the rings on the table, putting one at each place setting.
5. The story suggests inviting friends to make napkins rings with you and making the work a party.
6. Answers will vary. Possible answers include: challenging friends or family members to a napkin ring-designing competition or conducting a craft class for younger brothers or sisters and their friends to teach them how to make napkin rings.

Page 68

Answers for questions 2 and 5 will vary according to the answer given for question 1. Answers for questions 3 and 4 will also vary.

Page 69

A. 6, 3, 7, 5, 1, 4, 2

B.
1. Cut strips of paper $2\frac{1}{2}$" x $5\frac{1}{2}$" (6.5 cm x 14 cm).
2. Spread glue all over the outside of a cardboard ring.
3. Center a cardboard ring on a paper strip and wrap the paper around the ring.

C.
1. Decorate the outside of the ring.
2. Tuck a napkin into the ring.

Page 70

Materials and directions will vary but must be appropriate for the selected project.

Page 74

1. He thought that he was the wisest person in the land.
2. Everyone was afraid that he might use his magic to change them into something like a pig or a flowerpot.
3. She said that he couldn't change anything, not even a caterpillar into a butterfly, and that even her cow was smarter than he was.
4. The facts of the conversation changed each time it was passed on to another person. It finally came to say that the milkmaid had challenged the magician to a contest to see who was smarter, and that the winner of the contest would be named the next governor.
5. She was good-natured and thought that if people wanted her wisdom, she should share it.
6. She said that the magician couldn't even remember to put on his shoes before he went outside, and then he showed up at the contest with bare feet.

Page 75

1. governor
2. magician
3. shoemaker
4. blacksmith
5. innkeeper
6. milkmaid
7. baker
8. seamstress
9. teacher
10. farmer
11. carpenter
12. laundress

shoemaker, blacksmith, innkeeper, milkmaid

magician, milkmaid

teacher, carpenter, seamstress

Page 76

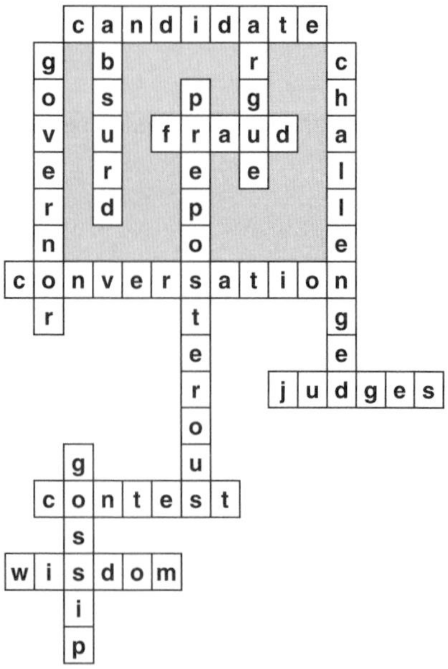

Page 77

Answers will vary. Possible answers include:

Magician
easily confused
forgetful
pompous
boastful
angry

Milkmaid
quick-thinking
self-assured
confident
good-natured

Both
ambitious
candidate for governor

Choices and explanations will vary, but explanations should include words and phrases listed in the Venn diagram.

Page 80

1. Chile
2. Answers will vary. Possible answers include: heading south, Andes Mountains, any of the names of cities or points of interest, skinny country, vicuña, Pacific Ocean, capital city Santiago, Strait of Magellan, Antarctica, South America
3. Answers will vary.
4. the Andes Mountains to the east, the Pacific Ocean to the west
5. The country has a variety of climates, and visitors can do many different kinds of activities.

Page 81

c, f, j, g, d, h, e, b, a, i

Answers may be any nine of the following compound words: swimsuit, sunscreen, icebergs, northeast, overhead, mountainsides, southwest, nearby, horseback, afternoon, breathtaking.

Sentences will vary. Examples:

I like to **swim** on hot days.

My dad bought a new **suit** to wear to his new job.

Her **swimsuit** was the first thing Susan packed for her trip to Hawaii.

Page 82

7	1
5	10
14	12
2	3
6	8
13	11
9	4

1. Arica, Antofagasta, Viña del Mar, Valparaíso, Puerto Montt
2. Santiago. It is in central Chile.
3. B
4. C

Page 83

Posters will vary but should show and tell about features of the country that were mentioned in the story.

Page 87

1. Muir devoted his life to learning about nature and botany, and he traveled many places to study the plants of those areas. Even when he was young, he would get up early to read or to invent things; he worked on his inventions even after working all day on the farm.
2. All parts of the machine were made of wood. The machine kept track of the hours, days, and months, and when it was time to get up in the morning, a rod tipped the bed to an upright position.
3. Answers may be any five of the following: farming, inventing, machine shop, sheepherding, working in a sawmill, studying plants and nature, writing
4. His articles in magazines and newspapers made many people aware of Yosemite Valley and its beauty. Among the people who visited the area were well-known politicians who used their power and influence to preserve the area's natural beauty by designating it a national park.
5. Answers will vary, but students should indicate that Muir was a good writer because his articles and books were popular and brought about the creation of national parks and forests.
6. Answers will vary.

Page 88

A. c, i, g, b, h, d, f, a, j, e

B. The words circled should be: ingenious, studious, hardworking, concerned, adventurous

C.
1. wilderness
2. stand
3. inventions

Page 89

A.
1. Scotland
2. Atlantic
3. Hudson, Erie, Great, Milwaukee
4. Fox, Wisconsin
5. Canada
6. Indiana, Mexico, California, Yosemite

B. **Bodies of Water:** Atlantic Ocean, Hudson River, Erie Canal, Great Lakes, Fox River, Gulf of Mexico

States: New York, Wisconsin, Indiana, California

Page 90

Answers will vary. Possible answers include:

Childhood: born in Scotland; had a strict father; went to live in America; worked on the family farm; liked to read, invent things, and learn about plants and birds

Travels: came to America, traveling through New York and across the Great Lakes to Wisconsin; went to Madison, Wisconsin, to exhibit his inventions; went to Canada to study botany; worked and studied plants in Indianapolis, Indiana; walked to the Gulf of Mexico; took a boat to California; worked, hiked, and climbed mountains in Yosemite Valley

Interest in Nature: made time to learn about nature and botany; went to Canada to study plants; walked 1,000 miles (1,609 km) to learn more about plants, people, and nature; hiked through and studied the mountains, glaciers, and valleys of California; cofounded the Sierra Club

Writings: wrote articles about nature for magazines and newspapers; wrote the books *The Mountains of California* and *Our National Parks*

Page 93

1. A powwow gathers many Native Americans together to honor the traditions of their ancestors and to share and enjoy the music, songs, dances, food, crafts, and customs of their heritage.
2. Many powwows are held just to celebrate life, but powwows may also be organized to celebrate special events, such as the birth of a child or a good harvest, or to honor special individuals, families, or groups.
3. The Drum is the most important element of a powwow. The entire powwow is organized around the Drum, which includes both the instrument and the singers and dancers who perform around it.
4. **arena:** drumming, singing (blanket song), dancing (war dance), contributing money, give-away ceremonies, honoring families, sharing gifts, contests for dancing, singing, and costumes

   crafts fair: arts and crafts for sale, elders sharing skills and stories, paintings and jewelry made of natural materials, playing traditional games, eating traditional foods
5. Before Europeans came to America, the lives of Native Americans were closely linked with nature. It provided their food, shelter, recreation, and everything else they needed in their daily lives. Native American religions also worshiped nature, and almost all things, living and nonliving, held some kind of spiritual meaning.

Page 94

A. d, i, e, g, b, j, c, a, k, l, h, f

B. 1. reservation
2. ceremonial
3. harvest
4. generation
5. respect

Page 95

1. Answers will vary.
2. Answers will vary.

Page 96

Festivals and plans will vary.

Page 100

1. He had made rules declaring that all the gold should belong to the greatest king in the universe and that he was the greatest king in the universe.
2. He thought that the moon was filled with gold, and when the phases of the moon made it appear to shrink, he thought someone was stealing the gold. He believed that a tower high enough to reach the moon could be built and that he could climb the tower to get the gold. When the king climbed the tower but was not high enough to reach the moon, he believed that a barrel could be moved from the bottom of the tower to the top to make the tower taller.
3. If the goatherd did not find a way for the king to reach the moon, the king would imprison the advisor along with the goatherd.
4. He had a dream in which he was standing on an old barrel to reach an apple that was high up in a tree.
5. Answers will vary. Students may say that the goatherd was clever because he knew all about goats and making cheese and because he knew that it was impossible to make the tower taller by taking something from the bottom and adding it to the top. Students may say that the goatherd was foolish for suggesting that a tower could be built to reach the moon.
6. Sentences will vary but should include something about the tower collapsing and taking the foolish king down with it.

Page 101

1. provide
2. impossible
3. universe
4. goatherd
5. command
6. proclaimed
7. entitled
8. treasury
9. telescope
10. crescent
11. royal
12. beyond
13. assume
14. declared
15. reasoned

Page 102

King Alexander

Problems:

thought gold was being stolen

needed help to reach the moon

still couldn't reach the moon

Solutions:

decided to catch the thief

sent his advisor to find the second-wisest person

demanded that something be taken from the bottom and added to the top

Royal Advisor

Problems:

had to find the second-wisest person

might get thrown into jail, too

Solutions:

came across two goatherds

helped the goatherd

Goatherd

Problem:

had to come up with a plan

Solution:

dreamed about picking fruit

Page 103

Retellings will vary.

Page 107

1. Answers will vary but should include some of the following details:

   Ruth Tall Chief: gave Maria opportunities to learn piano and ballet because she felt that music and dance should be part of her daughters' lives, and she wanted them to have careers on stage; decided that the family should move to California so her daughters would have a better chance for success

   Madame Nijinska: told Maria that she had talent but needed to start over to learn ballet correctly; made Maria work harder than ever to develop her talent; helped Maria see herself as a ballerina and choose ballet as a career

   George Balanchine: taught Maria to use her strengths and become a better dancer; invited her to join his company, which became very popular, making Maria more popular; featured Maria as a star performer

2. The share of money Alex Tall Chief received for oil found on the Osage reservation was enough to support his family.
3. Elizabeth Marie Tall Chief changed her first name to Maria and her last name to one word (Tallchief) after she finished high school and was invited to join and tour with the Ballet Russe de Monte Carlo.
4. She became a prima ballerina with the New York City Ballet and was with that company for 19 years (from 1946 to 1965).

Page 108

A. Answers will vary. Possible answers include: proud, graceful, famous, talented, determined, successful, popular, gifted, ambitious

B.

1. determined	6. awed
2. electrifying	7. bearing
3. original	8. company
4. retired	9. promise
5. strengths	10. ambition

Page 109

1. Answers will vary. Possible answers include:

   Performing Arts: singing, dancing, acting, mime, stand-up comedy

   Visual Arts: sculpture, pottery-making, photography, metalwork, jewelry-making
2. Answers will vary.
3. Answers will vary.
4. Artists and art forms will vary.

Page 110

A. Answers will vary. "Yes" answers should mention Maria's talent, love for ballet, and success as reasons. "No" answers might indicate that Maria may have been equally successful using her musical talent and that she should have explored a music career to some extent before making a final decision.

B. Personal choices and reasons will vary.

Page 114

1. He was probably nervous because everything was new and different and because he was only ten years old and had to spend the day with a stranger, away from his father.
2. at the Chinatown Neighborhood Center
3. Cheng's family probably eats a lot of seafood because it is sold at so many of the markets in Chinatown. Also, Cheng and Danny had seafood (prawns) for lunch that day, and they stopped to pick up fish for dinner.
4. Answers will vary but could include any four of the following:

   Danny learned...

   that Chinatown has a lot of outdoor markets.

   about styles of oriental art.

   about Chinese history and why so many Chinese people moved to America.

   where Chinatown started and how it grew.

   about the earthquake of 1906.

   the names of some Chinese foods and what those foods are.

   how fortune cookies are made.

   that the Chinese like to laugh, have fun, and even play bingo, just like people in any other culture.
5. Danny's curiosity and Cheng's eagerness to show him around Chinatown and introduce him to Chinese art, history, culture, and even his friends, are signs that the boys enjoyed their time together. They also smiled and laughed a lot and said that they both wanted to visit each other again sometime.
6. Cheng may want to visit Montana because, after showing Danny around his city, he probably wonders what life is like where Danny lives, and, since he and Danny got along so well, he would probably enjoy having Danny as a tour guide around his hometown in Montana.

Page 115

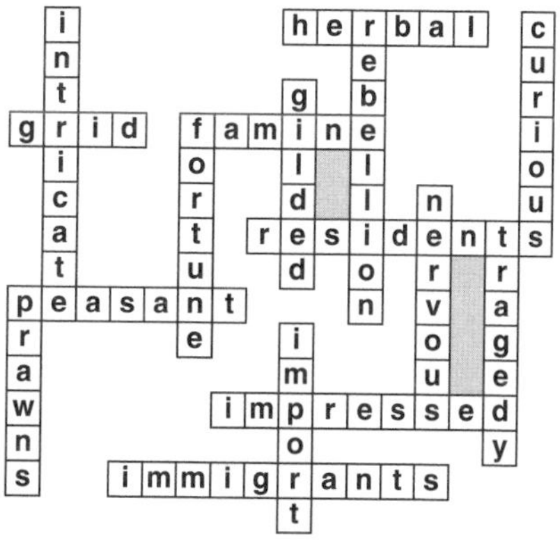

Page 116

Letters will vary but the places and activities mentioned must be reasonable and accurate for the letter writer's location.

Page 117

Places and activities will vary but the activities and explanation for each stop must be reasonable and accurate for that destination.

Page 120

1. His older brothers and sisters called him "J. C." (short for James Cleveland). A teacher, however, misunderstood "J. C." and wrote down "Jesse," and the name stayed with him throughout his life.
2. He tied the world record for the 100-yard dash and set new world records in the running broad jump and in the 220-yard hurdles.
3. Hitler was angry that black athletes had won medals. He had wanted the Olympics to help him prove that black athletes, like all black people, were inferior to the Germans.
4. Luz Long was the German athlete who won the silver medal in the broad jump at the 1936 Olympics. Even after losing the gold medal to Owens, Long befriended Owens and cheered his performance. In spite of Hitler's feelings toward the black athletes, Long put his arm around Owens in a public display of congratulations.
5. Blacks had to sit in the back of buses and were not allowed to live in many neighborhoods or eat at many restaurants. They also were not given the same honors and recognition as white people were given for their achievements.
6. The Medal of Freedom was Owens's highest honor. He received this award in 1976.

Page 121

A.

1. hurdles	7. professional
2. exhibitions	8. formally
3. recognized	9. sophomore
4. compete	10. inferior
5. discrimination	11. consultant
6. befriended	12. legendary

B.

1. friend	4. profession
2. consult	5. exhibit
3. legend	6. discriminate

Page 122

Answers will vary but should include some of the following ideas:

1. In track and field events, Owens set a world record in the 220-yard hurdles race. He also overcame many personal hurdles during his life. As a young boy, he worked with the rest of his family to overcome poverty. To be successful in school and sports, he had to find time to study, practice, and compete, and, in college, he even had to support a wife. He worked hard at everything. He even competed in track meets when he was injured. As a black American, he had to overcome discrimination, even in the United States and even after he had become famous. And when he didn't earn enough as an athlete, he took other jobs, including being a janitor and a disk jockey.
2. Olympic medals recognize only the athletes' hard work and abilities in their chosen sports. The Medal of Freedom and the Living Legend Award recognize all of a person's skills and accomplishments, as well as how that person contributes to society. These two awards recognized Owens not just as an outstanding athlete but as an outstanding person. Besides athletic achievements, Owens was also a successful businessman and public speaker, and he shared his success and his time with others, particularly with young people to help them make their dreams of success come true.

Page 123

Content of personal narratives will vary but must include appropriate requirements for meeting the specified goal(s) or achievement(s) and the obstacles that might be faced.

Page 126

1. The location is on the Gulf of Mexico, because Abuelita stares across the gulf toward Mexico, her homeland. The language in the story suggests that it's set in modern times.
2. The dog had a toothache, and Abuelita accidentally hurt him.
3. Mrs. Bass seems very attached to General and seems to depend on him for companionship. She was very concerned about why General was not eating. She was fearful that he had a grave illness, and was extremely relieved to learn that he may only have a toothache.
4. David thinks that Abuelita doesn't trust Mrs. Bass because Mrs. Bass doesn't speak Spanish. Some students may also understand that there are many other cultural differences that might have made Abuelita uncomfortable or insecure around Mrs. Bass.
5. When Mrs. Bass thanked Abuelita for finding out what was wrong with General, Abuelita said "you are welcome" to Mrs. Bass in English.
6. Accept any reasonable answer, but most students will predict that Mrs. Bass will take General to the vet and that she and Abuelita will become friends. Some may predict that Abuelita will overcome her negative feelings toward English-speaking people and make other friends.

Page 127

Answers will vary. Possible answers include:

1. stomped, thudded
2. shook, jiggled
3. looked, gazed
4. crumpled, creased
5. pulled, yanked
6. section, length
7. cry, whine
8. shrill, squeaky

1. *abuelita*
2. *sí*
3. *creo que sí*
4. *gracias*

Page 128

Answers will vary.

Page 129

1. Texas, Louisiana, Mississippi, Alabama, Florida
2. Texas, north and east
3. Galveston, Pensacola, Tampa
4. Florida
5. Rio Grande, Mississippi River

Page 133

1. He wanted to bring something from his own heritage for the class melting pot, but because he was adopted, he didn't know anything about his biological parents or his family background.
2. He probably wanted to know about his own heritage after hearing Mrs. Grill talk about the ancestors and backgrounds of Americans from various cultures, and he wanted to be able to share his own heritage with his classmates.
3. Carlos had been adopted by his biological grandparents, and although he didn't live with his parents, he knew who they were and had contact with them.
4. They could add something that was from a culture they admired.
5. The United States is sometimes called a "melting pot" because its inhabitants come from so many different countries and cultures.
6. Tom realized that he is made up of different people he has known or has contact with each day.

Page 134

Possible answers include:

A.
1. *Melting pot* refers to the blending of many different cultures into a single society or group.
2. *Recent arrivals* means those who came to a place the shortest amount of time ago.
3. *Tom's out* refers to an acceptable way for him to complete the homework assignment without needing to know anything about his true background or heritage.
4. *Out of the picture* means "no longer part of a certain situation."
5. *Biological parents* are a person's birth parents.
6. *Adoptive parents* are people who use legal means to make a person their son or daughter.
7. *That last addition* refers to the frog (the last item put into the kettle).

B.
1. enthusiasm
2. culture
3. keepsake
4. mesh
5. sullen
6. heritage
7. knickknacks
8. comment

Page 135

Answers will vary, but all answers should mention the people and events Tom had seen or experienced the previous day.

Page 136

1. Answers will vary.
2. Answers will vary.

Page 140

1. The game is a conversation in which the girl and her great-grandmother take turns talking about their lives and comparing things that happened when the great-grandmother was ten years old to similar events in the girl's life today.
2. Answers can be any of the following: the invention of air conditioning; the cost of things; the sizes of homes and schools; local, low-tech music concerts from a bandwagon on the street to crowded, high-tech concerts; cars and buses took the place of horses and wagons; automatic washing machines replaced manual washboards; indoor plumbing replaced outhouses; electric refrigerators replaced iceboxes; children's chores are now fewer and easier; home remedies for illnesses changed to medicines; and pastimes such as sewing, baking, and gardening were replaced by watching television and playing video games.
3. Grandma Bonnie helped her father chop wood and do farm work and helped her mother sew, cook, and do laundry. Her granddaughter helped her mother in the garden one summer, and she sometimes bakes cookies and puts clothes into the washing machine.
4. The girl knew that she and her great-grandmother would do some kind of project together because Grandma Bonnie always ended the story game by telling the girl something that her father (the girl's great-great-grandfather) had taught her to do, and when the girl asks Grandma Bonnie to show her how, the answer is always "yes."

Page 141

1. *adv.* extremely; extraordinarily
2. *v.* supplied with the necessary materials to do a particular job
3. *adj.* relating to a gas that is used mainly in tubular electric lights
4. *n.* a corrugated metal board against which wet, soapy clothes are rubbed to make them clean
5. *adj.* puffy, swollen-looking, or rising in a mass into the air
6. *adv.* certainly; without a doubt
7. *v.* to force air from the throat through a liquid held in the mouth, causing a gurgling sound
8. *n.* a toilet, especially an outdoor toilet, or "outhouse"
9. *adj.* relating to or containing herbs

Page 142

A. Questions will vary.

B. Answers will vary.

Page 143

Accept any reasonable answers for present-day information. Answers for "Then" will depend on the age of the person. Possible answers include:

Communication: (now) cordless phones, cell phones, computers (e-mail, Skype®, etc.); (then) letters, dial telephones, telegrams

Transportation: (now) hybrid automobiles, high-speed rail, jet aircraft; (then) cars, buses, trains, propeller airplanes

Recreation: (now) electronic games, DVDs, surfing the Internet; (then) television, radio, playing outdoors

Page 145

1. A
2. Answers should include information similar to the following:

   Setting:
   Where in the World? takes place over several days and includes many locations throughout the country of Chile. *Cheng Wan's Visitor* takes place in a single day and has one main location (Chinatown).

   Characters:
   In *Where in the World?* the two main characters are the narrator and the reader. In *Cheng Wan's Visitor*, the two main characters are fictional (Cheng and Danny).

   Action:
   The characters in *Where in the World?* hike, swim, fly, and sail from place to place, and the focus is on each area's geographical location and features. In *Cheng Wan's Visitor,* the characters walk from place to place and the focus is mainly historical and cultural.
3. a. B
   b. A
   c. B
   d. A
   e. A
   f. B
4. Answers will vary.

Page 146

1. C
2. Answers will vary but must include a lesson of some kind. Accept any reasonable response.
3. Answers will vary but should include ideas similar to the following: Their achievements both required natural talent, physical strength, many years of hard work, and competing with others for the top position. Also, both Tallchief and Owens had to face and overcome discrimination to reach their goals, and they both became famous throughout the world.
4. Answers will vary, but students will most likely say that Jesse Owens had a more difficult time. He came from a poorer family than Maria Tallchief and appeared to have more responsibilities to juggle (studying, practicing, competing, a wife to support). He was also discriminated against both in the United States and Europe, whereas Maria Tallchief seemed to be well-received in Europe and suffered discrimination to a lesser degree than Owens in the United States.
5. Answers will vary but must be well supported. The adjectives *determined* and *strong* seem to apply equally to both Tallchief and Owens, while *legendary* may be better suited to Owens and *proud* may be better suited to Tallchief. Accept any reasonable answer.

Page 147

1. *The Warrior and the Princess* is a legend that explains how the mountain Ixtaccihuatl ("The Sleeping Woman") in Mexico and the nearby volcano Popocatepetl ("Smoking Mountain") came to exist.
2. *The One-Inch Boy*: b, c, j, k, l
   The Warrior and the Princess:
   d, g, i
   Both: a, e, f, h
3. Prince Popo warned the emperor of invaders and bravely led troops against the emperor's enemies, saving the kingdom.

   One-Inch Boy proved himself to his parents by successfully completing his journey to Kyoto and making his fortune, and he proved himself to the noble by saving the great man's daughter from the ogre.

Page 148

1. B
2. **food:** Traditional foods, such as fry bread, are available at a powwow. Besides serving special holiday foods for Tet, food is placed on an altar with candles and incense to share with the spirits of ancestors.

   music: The Drum (both the instrument and the singers and dancers that perform around it) are the lifeblood of a powwow. In Vietnam, small villages often celebrate Tet with the traditional songs and dances of their regions.

   decorations: The dancers at a powwow wear colorful costumes with beads, bells, feathers, and bright designs. Some also paint their skin with beautiful designs. For Tet, people decorate their homes with spring blossoms and hang banners and lights outdoors. They also place pictures of ancestors, along with candles and incense, on an altar inside the home.

   why celebrated: A powwow is a celebration of life, culture, and pride. Tet is a time to remember ancestors and to welcome spring.
3. Checked items should be music and dancing, special foods, gift-giving, games and contests. You may decide to accept other responses if details from the story justify them.
4. Choices will vary, but accurate details from the stories must be included in the answer.

Page 149

1. a. both e. ants
   b. birds f. ants
   c. both g. birds
   d. ants h. birds
2. Both homes are made of mud, but the homes of South American rainforest ants are built on tree branches and flamingos' homes are mounds of mud on the ground.
3. Accept any reasonable and accurate answer. Possible answers include:

   Because individual ants are so small, millions of them live and work together to survive.

   Different species of birds have beaks, feet, feathers, and other physical features that help them find and eat the kinds of foods available in their environments and build homes suitable for their environments.